Angelina

Be careful what you wish for…

by **A G Hansell**

Novels by A G Hansell

A Novel World: Before
Angelina

Angelina

by A G Hansell

Published by Satellite Publications

Edited by Julie Helliwell, Linnea Hunt-Stewart, & ACH

Book design by the HAG

Cover design by Buzz Erlinger-Ford

Production management by the HAG

ISBN 978-87-93696-17-4

The BITS Inspector® is a registered UK trademark.

For information about gaining rights to reproduce any excerpts from this work, write to info@satellitepublications.com

Ever done something you knew you shouldn't?
Ever thought something you wish you hadn't?
Ever dreamt something you daren't tell?

Watch out.
Angelina's coming for you.

For all those who've suffered, and everyone who will.

Dedicated to ... oh ... let's not tempt fate.

CONTENTS

PROLOGUE

Fifty years ago

Angelina sighs. She tears her eyes away from Grandad Maksim's portrait, mostly ignoring the patch of unfaded wallpaper over the empty space beside it. *Rot in hell, you bastard!* Nostrils flaring, memory flashes of blood's bitter taste turn her tongue dry.

She gulps down her vodka.

"Boris, where are you?" she says, her tone harsher than she'd typically use with him.

Boris opens the door and steps into the room. "Where I always am. At your back."

Angelina rolls her eyes, and Boris grins. She studies him. "You were watching?"

The question lingers in the slightly musky air, giving Boris time to think. "The whisky?"

A curt nod.

"Yes. The whole thing," Boris says.

Angelina's eyes pop wide open. "All of it? How?"

"Doc." A thrust of his chin.

Angelina glances at Doc, lips parting a little. Raising his eyebrows slightly, Doc shrugs, a small smile barely visible on his lips. Angelina shakes her head while looking back at Boris. "And you did nothing?"

"I am *your* bodyguard, Angelina, no one else's. And I've been *yours* since before you were born."

One Hundred Years Ago and More

One hundred and four years ago

Endless, torturous screams escape the inadequate walls of the delivery room, screeching down the hallways as if, by vanishing, they might offer comfort to the woman they came from. Maksim and Valery sit side by side. Valery, eyes cast down, tries not to be noticed. Maksim fidgets constantly, crossing and uncrossing his legs, leaning back, head against the wall, then chin in palms, elbows resting on knees.

The wide white doors remain closed between them and the suffering, expectant woman. A nurse runs out a side door, head down. She steals a glance at the two men before hurrying in the other direction.

"I should've forced the operation on her," Maksim says, angrily spitting out the words.

Valery doesn't know what to say. *Hard to arrange something like that.* But his father's an expert at illegal, so that wouldn't have prevented him if he'd chosen to do it. Valery's sure that any response would be wrong, given the circumstances. So, he says nothing and hopes he'll not suffer for his silence.

There are many reasons why Valery pities the ex-prostitute howling in the delivery room, giving birth to his half-sister. But he's never talked about them with his father and doesn't dare mention his feelings now. Valery usually only speaks to his father when spoken to in a manner that demands a reply. Even with Valery's thirty years, Maksim still sees him as a boy, not old enough to comprehend life's trials despite his suffering.

"And I should never have fallen in love with the wench," Maksim says.

Valery's eyes open wide, but he keeps his head down.

"I should've sent her back on the streets where she belongs."

The screaming subsides temporarily as if the laboring woman is considering how to punish Maksim for his hurtful words.

"You can't stop yourself falling in love, can you?" Valery blurts out before thinking.

Maksim twists his head sideways to look at his son and raises an eyebrow.

He's asking, what do you know about it? Valery thinks. But then Maksim poses the question quite differently.

"Have you ever been in love, Valery? And I don't mean flings. Really in love?"

Valery blushes, surprised. He feels his cheeks burn and has to think about how best to answer. "Maybe one time, when I was much younger," he says, looking away. "More infatuation than love, I guess. It happened so fast I couldn't stop it." He chooses each word carefully. "But I grew out of it soon enough."

Valery recalls the nights he spent forcing himself to stop crying. He gave up, though, and even today, he silently cries every night in bed. He doesn't mention that he still thinks of her every day. And in his heart, at least, he remains faithful to her, even though she left him.

Maksim blinks his eyes wide open and stares at Valery. "What was her name?"

Valery lowers his head, eyes racing around, catching imaginary dots flashing on the floor. "It's not important. Long past now."

"There's hope for you yet, son," Maksim says with a weary smile and lays his enormous hand on Valery's shoulder.

Valery fights the urge to wince and pull away.

For the first twenty years of Valery's life, the primary correction for any misdoing had been a smack of some sort. The older Valery became, the harder Maksim struck, until one day, Valery lost his already short temper. He swung back at his father, punching him squarely on the jaw and knocking him backward. But despite Valery's incredible size, strength, and speed, youth was against him, and the inexperienced blow wasn't enough to seriously hurt the giant man, regardless of Valery's training or Maksim's advancing years.

Maksim was never one to lose face, even in front of his son, so he smacked Valery to the ground and kept beating him until Valery conceded. Yet since that day, Maksim hasn't raised a hand to him.

Upon realizing the change in his father, Valery had forcefully reconditioned his primal defense reaction: The wincing angered his father and made Valery feel even more pathetic. Valery often wondered why that one retaliatory punch was enough to end his father's lifetime pattern of violent discipline.

Maybe the realization that one day I'd beat him was the best reason Valery had thought of. And that was partially correct.

Maksim had started Valery's training from infancy. There was much to learn if he were to take over from Maksim. And yes, Maksim brought the boy up to be tough—that was true enough—because being hard was a fundamental element of success in crime. But Maxim also tried to avoid making an enemy of his son and turning him into a bitter, angry monster by encouraging Valery's academic skills.

Once Valery showed spirit enough to fight back against his father, Maksim thought it was time to build up that spirit instead of knocking him down. He intensified Valery's scholarly program and rewarded his efforts by introducing him more to the business. He also initiated a grueling physical training schedule so he could take on men Maksim's size, should that ever prove necessary. Valery had to learn how to fight to kill with his bare hands, the way Maksim's father taught him. The way Maksim took his revenge on those who murdered Valery's mother.

He'll never know that Mom's death wrecked my first true love, and probably my last, Valery thinks, furious now that Maksim has reminded him. Valery holds his father responsible for both events: His mother died because of his father's life of crime, and his first love left him after reading the headlines and hearing the rumors. He had no evidence, neither for the slaying of his beloved mother nor for his beloved deserting him. He didn't need proof. Valery knew his father was to blame. But Valery kept his thoughts locked away, and he never dared to search out the truth, especially after realizing he couldn't recall his beloved's name.

The nurse returns, half running, half walking beside a serious-looking white-coated man, the lead OB-GYN. He asks her a question. She shakes her head. The nurse's loose eyes can't resist, and she takes another quick peek at Valery and Maksim before disappearing again through the side door.

As the howling from the delivery chamber rips through the hospital wing once more, Maksim breaks his words to use the relative silences of the gasps and breaths between the screams.

"Alena. She'll be called Alena. She wants that. If the girl is born at night...

"One meaning is 'moon,' she says. I checked. It's not obvious, but she likes it."

Again, no response from Valery, except for a slight affirmative nod.

Hour after hour, they sit, exchanging small talk now and then, mostly in one direction, accompanied by sporadic head shakes, nods, shrugs, and the like.

The tension grows. Not between them but niggling its way into their crawling bones. The woman's screaming is hard to bear; her pain must surely be insufferable.

After more than six long hours and medics running in and out through the side door, the lead OB-GYN stands before Maksim and Valery with downturned lips and burdened weary brow. Maksim stands, stares directly into the man's eyes and sees the fact of the matter etched in his gaze.

Valery sees it too, and usually unsure of what to expect when it comes to his father's reaction, he braces himself for the worst.

"Your daughter is safe but suffering from her horrendous struggle," the doctor says. "I'm afraid her mother had severe complications. She agreed to let us save the baby, but I'm sorry to tell you that she didn't survive the birth. I'm so sorry for your loss."

"What the hell do you mean she didn't make it?" Maksim yells as he shoves the doctor aside and storms into the delivery room. He charges up to the dead woman lying on the table, swipes the cover from her head and shoulders, then stops and stares. He's used to seeing death in all its forms, but rarely in someone he cares for.

Valery follows his father into the room, staying behind him, out of his way. He quietly but urgently motions to the remaining medics, ensuring they don't hang around. Concerned for their own wellbeing, the staff don't wait for a second warning: These men's reputations precede them.

Throughout the poor dead woman's terrible struggle, hearing her screams change in volume, length, and strength, reducing to desperate weak screeches over the long hours, Maksim's tears had unwillingly started gathering. And in preparation for their long, infrequent journey to the surface, they began welling up from deep within when he saw the truth in the doctor's eyes. Now, he reaches down to take her hand. He feels her life force deserted and shivers as death's cold sets in deeper, despite his warmth. And finally, they break. A few tears, two, maybe three. But there's no one close enough to notice or care.

They both stand, staring, Maksim alone, mourning his love, now passed, Valery looking at his father's broad back, not knowing what to do until the OB-GYN silently steps back into the room. Visible only to Valery, he points at the baby.

"She needs some attention," the doctor says into Valery's ear. "The birth was hard on her. We don't want her to suffer more than she already has." *Or will do with you lot.*

"Tata, the doctor says Alena needs caring for. She needs the nurses," Valery says, speaking gently but firmly. Sounding weak or miserable would only irritate Maksim.

Hearing Alena's name drags Maksim back from his thoughts, and he folds the cloth back over his dead woman, then steps over to the OB-GYN. "Sorry, Doctor," he says, looking directly at him.

The OB-GYN meets Maksim's gaze with soft, steady eyes and nods slightly, pressing his closed lips into a conciliatory half-turned-down smile. If he's intimidated by this notorious boss standing before him, he certainly hides it well.

"So, what's next?" Maksim asks.

"Well, she must stay under observation for a few days. If you're ready to see her, you should do it now. Five minutes only, I'm afraid. Then we'll take her into our care, and you can go home and rest," the man says. "I'm sure it's been quite an ordeal. We'll call you tomorrow to discuss how to move forward."

For a few thoughtful moments, Maksim looks at the cot where his newborn daughter lies and then walks over to her. Valery follows, curious; he's never seen a newborn up close before. He's never had a sister before.

Reaching out his massive hands, Maksim stops and looks up at the doctor. A simple nod of approval is enough. Maksim picks up the baby and lays her on his thick forearm while lifting her to his chest. He stares into Alena's wide eyes, his open, smiling mouth and uplifted cheeks conflicting with his squinting expression and tilting, questioning head.

Peering down at the girl and tickling her palm with his pinky finger, which she grabs, Valery exerts every ounce of self-control he can muster to contain a surprised gasp. The nurses have washed Alena well; her skin is fair but slightly flushed. Blonde-haired with big, black shining eyes, she smiles back at her brother as if he'd just handed her the biggest treat of her young life.

In awe and wonder, swept off his feet by her beauty and innocence, Valery smiles without restraint. Losing control for a moment, he slips up and looks at his father. "She's like an angel," he whispers.

"She is," Maksim says, glancing at Valery with love in his eyes for the first time in decades, a love that has blinded him, and he fails to see the look in his son's eyes before turning back to Alena. Maksim only has eyes for his daughter. Yet maybe some primal instinct triggers deep inside him, for he pulls Alena closer.

Valery notices but shows no sign, yet in that momentary reaction, he decides, *she'll be mine regardless.* As he stares at his half-sister, a vague idea starts to form in his mind. *She'll turn to me because I'll be the one who takes care of her. And I will protect her. And finally, I won't be all alone.*

After the nurses take Alena away and check the telephone number they should call the next day, Maksim says, "Let's go home. I need a drink."

Who cares that it's four in the morning, Valery tells himself. "I could use one, too," he says. *I want to celebrate.*

Fighting Talk

Leaning farther and farther forward in his seat, Valery casts sideways glances at his father to determine his state. He relaxes after seeing Maksim's half-closed eyes and head resting against the car's cushioned doorframe. As the old man snoozes, his head bobs back and forth in rhythm with the vehicle's motion.

Valery's huge hand clasps a heavy whisky tumbler resting securely on his thigh. The car's gentle jostling on the firm suspension and the heating—furiously fighting off the first bitter cold of winter—make Valery drowsy. He leans his head back on the seat's headrest and closes his eyes.

"You're waving about all over the place, boy! Are you trying to fly?" Maksim says as he slaps Valery across one cheek.

Valery's head jerks to one side, and he turns his gaze to the floor.

Grabbing the small pistol out of Valery's hand, Maksim deftly removes the magazine. "You're not finished yet. You need to do that again."

A single tear runs down Valery's cheek.

"Hold your arms out straight, boy, and firm. You know how this works," Maksim says, shoving the reloaded gun back into Valery's hand. "Seven rounds. Don't stop until it's empty." He waves his hand toward the target at the far end of the specially built indoor shooting range at the back of the house.

Valery does as he's told, as he always does. He shoots.

BANG!

He flinches. Forces himself not to close his eyes. But he whimpers. A brief, involuntary, childish sound.

"Again!"

Valery fires.

"Again!"

BANG!

This new pistol is heavier and much louder than his first. Violent. The recoil, fierce. Clenching his jaw, Valery tries to steady his shaking chin. He cries, unable to stop himself. The boy whimpers again, and the tears flow from his brimming eyes.

"Again!" Maksim shouts.

Valery shoots. Each explosive blast seems louder than the last, and this time, Valery shudders and squeezes his eyes closed. He fires again, over and over, until the magazine is empty. He misses his target every time.

"Pathetic," Maksim says while slapping Valery across the side of his head. He snatches the gun from Valery. "Every day, we'll do this, until every shot hits the center ring. Now, get to the gym, boy."

The training gym is two doors down the corridor, and in no time, Valery has almost finished laying out the mats, as he does every day. Some days, he trains with his father, sometimes with his trainer.

As Valery puts the last mat in place, a blinding pain shoots through his back between his shoulders, and he flies forward. His body crashes onto the soft training pads, but he lands face-first on the hardwood floor.

Stars explode in Valery's eyes, and he cries out as he hears a cracking sound coming from his nose. Blood drips on his T-shirt, running through his fingers as he rolls onto his side, cupping his nose and crying.

"Clumsy boy. Get up! And stop that wailing," Maksim says, grabbing his son's arm and yanking him to his feet. "I've told you a million times, never turn your back on your enemy."

Maksim pulls Valery's head back to inspect the boy's face. "Hmmm," he says, studying Valery's broken nose. Then he clamps the nose between his index and middle finger and twists it hard.

"Argh!" Valery shouts, then starts crying again.

Glowering while speaking, Maksim says, "I said stop sniveling."

"Why are you so angry?" Valery yells. To a bystander, it might look like he would scream in his father's face if he were tall enough.

"Don't answer me back, boy!" Maksim says, and in a further explosion of frustration, he slaps Valery onto the mats just as Angeli walks in. Valery curls up and covers his bleeding nose with his hands.

"Maksim, for God's sake. He's only eight," Angeli says while rushing to her son. "You're being too hard on him." She squats and reaches out to stroke Valery's face.

"And you're being too soft on him," Maksim says, bending down and grabbing Angeli's wrist. His tone is low, almost a growl, his cheeks flushed.

"Let go of me!" she says and slaps his face. The blow is awkward but hard and clearly heard in the large room.

With eyes wide and mouth half-open, Maksim drops Angeli's wrist, but he instinctively whirls into a back-handed response. Yet somehow, there's restraint, and he only clips Angeli's cheek with his knuckles. But the light blow and her flinching withdrawal are enough to knock her off balance, backward off the mats, and she lands heavily on the hard wooden floor.

"Ow!"

"Oh, my love, I'm so sorry," he says and goes to her, stretching out his arms to help her up.

She holds him off with outstretched palm. "Leave me alone. Go and call that young doctor. Get him out here to look at Valery. He owes you a favor or two."

Maksim straightens, hesitates, and looks from his wife to his boy.

Valery crawls over to his mother. "Are you OK?" he whispers.

"I'm fine," Angeli says as she hugs Valery and gently kisses his head. A fierce anger burns in her eyes, and her lip curls up, but her husband can't see all that.

Maksim glares at the boy before storming from the gym.

The car's right wheels slam into a deep pothole in the road, and Valery's head knocks against the window, the whisky sloshing around in the glass on his knee. Lost in his memories in the warmth, Valery had almost dozed off. He sits up slightly and straightens his head, raising it off the headrest.

"Were you asleep?" Maksim says.

Valery opens his eyes and watches the drive's wide double gates slide open, left and right, on their sturdy supporting wheels. "No. Just resting my eyes."

Mutual Loss

The Belarusian mansion and grounds are worlds apart from the gray concrete streets and bleak off-white hospital walls where Maksim left Alena and her dead mother. Staring out the car's windscreen, Valery imagines his sister playing croquet on the well-kept lawns, her slender young legs exposed under a frilly, summery skirt, perfect knees slightly bent as she lines up her mallet for a stop shot. He holds his breath as Alena squats to check her aim, a flash of white panties covering her crotch. Valery remains frozen until he's shaken off those loose thoughts.

The long line of luxurious limos pulls up outside the residence, the cars, a trademark of Maksim's mysterious family. Matte black from bumper to bumper and roof to tarmac, it's impossible to see where the windows meet the doors' metal or to know that the vehicles' exteriors consist solely of bulletproof materials. All seven cars look identical, thus hiding the exact location of any VIP passengers.

A footman opens a door. Father and son clasp thick fingers around their heavy-cut lead crystal tumblers while stepping from one of the luxury vehicles. The sloshing amber liquid glows brightly through the sharply cut angles as the glass picks up harsh rays of light from the lamps lighting up the driveway. During the twenty-five-minute journey from the hospital, the two men knocked back two ample rounds and are well into a large third as they arrive home. But they've only just begun.

Reaching the relative privacy of their enormous sitting room, Maksim can finally relax. He looks old and weary as he settles into a chaise longue and puts up his feet.

"Ah, that's better," he says. Even his sigh sounds spent. "Valery, would you do the honors?" he says, holding out his empty tumbler. "I'll have vodka."

Valery prepares more drinks. The clinking of glasses and bottles on the marble bar mingles with the gentle clacks of warm and cold snack plates as the family's staff set food on the low glass table close to Maksim.

Alone again, they sit quietly, Valery in a huge leather armchair, Maksim on his long sofa, both consumed by their thoughts. A tall old grandfather clock stands against a far wall, ticking steadily. The only other sounds breaking the silence are the two men drinking, and pouring, until, well into a newly breached decanter of vodka, Maksim speaks.

"Do you remember when I first met her? I fell in love with her immediately, you know," he says, suddenly realizing he's reliving a conversation that took place decades ago, in another time and place. The liquor, lack of sleep, and old age are taking their toll: Valery is not Alex.

Valery doesn't look at his father while answering. "I remember. It was sixteen years ago, on your sixtieth birthday and the tenth anniversary of your rise to power. Quite a party," Valery says, his tone almost flat.

"Yes, one hell of an affair," Maksim says, noticing Valery didn't spot his mistake. Maksim doesn't bother correcting himself, and they both fall back into their own worlds of things past and things yet to come.

Of course, Maksim realizes. *He thinks I'm asking about Alena's mother. And he has no idea someone attacked us again the day I met* her. *And that if they'd succeeded, they'd probably have murdered us all,* Maksim thinks. *Nobody had suspected Pavel as the next one who'd challenge me for my head; my godson, goddammit, my best friend's son.*

Pavel refused to believe Alex forced my hand, that I had to take his father's life to defend my own. Bitterness poisons everything, doesn't it? Poisoned the father, poisoned the son.

Ah, Alex, my friend, Maksim thinks, sensing now that his anger is long past. He's unaware of when that happened. *Why couldn't you just let nature take its course? The strongest usually comes out on top.*

Twenty-six years ago, five years after his father's death and the subsequent years of careful, secretive, and complex planning, Maksim surprised everyone when he performed his remarkable multi-coup. He took out all the bosses in Belarus and five of the eight most powerful in Ukraine, effectively elevating himself to the powerful position of boss of bosses across both countries.

Maksim then leaked anonymous tips implicating the remaining top bosses in capital crimes, and he gloated with satisfaction as the cops locked away all three bosses within the year. Their sentences fell, and in the six months that followed, Maksim had the bosses assassinated in their cells, then he swooped in and took their territories. He crushed any remaining bosses of standing in Ukraine within the following three years.

The key to Maksim's success was to make his move secretively and maintain anonymity in his new role as the boss of bosses. Maksim had created multiple new identities for himself and his family so they could slip in and out of different fictitious lives as needed. *Hah! All that elaborate scheming. My death fooled 'em all. Damned disguises confused even me,* he used to sit and think in the solitude of his office, silently chuckling to himself.

Only one of the original bosses knew Maksim's true identity because he was the only one spared the chance of life. Alex had been Maksim's best friend since they were small boys.

Alex's father had been Maksim's father's best friend since their days in prison together.

One year after Maksim's birth, Russian soldiers working under the Gulag administration dragged Maksim's father, at age twenty-five, brutally from his home. They imprisoned him for the next thirteen years of his life, until Stalin's reign ended. Maksim's father's fellow inmates indoctrinated him into a bloody and vicious life of crime, and, being an exceptionally clever young man, he quickly learned the ropes of survival. Maksim's father befriended Alex's father in their first year of confinement. Together, by combining their wit, strength, and unwavering loyalty to each other, and by the grace of some greater power, they persevered where millions did not.

But camp life also forever damaged and scarred them. So, when they finally emerged as bitter and angry survivors from the grasp of hell, they charged through life like a two-headed soulless monster, exploring freedom in a world of mostly lesser monsters and their prey. Such a bond, written under the fiery shadows of the Gates of Hades and likely sealed by the Lord of Darkness himself, forged in blood and tested through terror, is not broken lightly. And a token—a resemblance—of that bond passed on from those inseparable lifelong friends to their sons, Maksim and Alex.

Ah, Alex, Maksim thinks again as his thoughts—for the umpteenth time— return to that horrible evening. *If only we'd known the same loyalty that our fathers knew.*

Is it really so that something exceptionally good can only come from something exceptionally bad? he asks himself again. *Is it only from suffering that true loyalty is born?*

Maksim sees their last argument before his eyes as if it had happened earlier this evening.

"Do you remember when I first met her? I fell in love with her immediately, you know," Maksim says to Alex, putting his glass on the table. "Life will never be the same without her. Those bastards! I killed every last one of them with my bare hands for taking her away from me."

"You also took something from *them*," Alex says, his tone bitter as he returns to their earlier conversation.

Still angry, Maksim thinks. "That's our line of work, Alex. Taking. And they were getting lazy, fat, sleepy. More importantly, they endangered us all with their sloppiness. They could've seen me coming if they'd stayed alert," he says.

"But you did all that without me. And now you expect me to work for you?" Alex yells at Maksim. "We were equal before. Friends! But now you think you own me? Command me? What made you think that you could be boss of all bosses?" Alex asks.

"Because I can," Maksim says. "I am. It was easy to take advantage of the rivalry. I just added to their confusion and turned their disorder to my advantage. They offered me no real opposition."

"I was already organizing things," Alex says again, his rising voice instilling false self-confidence, his growing temper turning conversation into confrontation.

Maksim had invited him to discuss a leading position in his new organization, but he knew Alex wouldn't see it as a positive move.

"You weren't having much success," Maksim argues gently, not wishing to provoke Alex further. "Thirty dead, almost equal numbers on both sides. That's more like wiping each other out than building something."

"Twelve of mine, eighteen of Dmitriy's. That's not equal numbers," Alex shouts.

And so they continue, Alex's anger increasing, Maksim becoming warier, until Alex does what Maksim feared he would—and pulls out a gun.

But even before Alex wraps a finger around the trigger, blood seeps from a hole between his eyes, trickling steadily but slowly, as if unwilling to accept the passing of life.

I'm glad I didn't risk my life like that with all the others, Maksim thinks, recalling his only thought immediately after shooting Alex. Then, looking at Valery, Maksim raises his glass and washes the memory away.

Two more unhappy losers tried to rid Maksim of the burden of life following his climb to power. One year before Alex's attempt, the first attack came six years after Maksim's coup and surprised everyone because it was unexpected, unplanned, and, as a result, uncoordinated and unsuccessful.

But it left its eternal marks, Maksim thinks, looking back. He's always had an acute memory for moments of danger and violence as if they were video recordings stored in his mind and ready to play on demand.

Walking down the hilly path from his father's grave toward the car park by the cemetery exit below, Maksim and his men hear noises behind them and turn to see men charging from behind the trees lining the path. The sun shines from behind the hill and blinds Maksim, but he makes out the leading man's jawline and build, and he's sure he sees the recognizable pinstripe of the suits he always wears.

Dmitriy! Maksim thinks. *I can almost smell the vodka on the man's breath.* He had a reputation for it.

Dmitriy had become convinced that this newcomer, living in the fancy mansion on the edge of the rich part of town, was none other than the new boss of all bosses *and* the supposedly dead Maksim himself. Dmitriy said the house sale after Maksim's death was a cover-up. No one believed him.

Finally, after years of trying to convince his associates of his theory, they spent the previous night drinking and debating. Unexpectedly, they'd found themselves angrily riling each other up, coaxing and cajoling toward Maksim's execution. When they realized that the rising sun heralded this stranger's yearly visit to the grave of the supposedly dead Maksim's father, they foolishly agreed that this would be a better time than most. They made hasty preparations, called in extra men and firepower, and deployed around the graveyard.

"Angeli, take Valery," Maksim says. "Run to the car," and he motions to three men to help cover them.

But Dmitriy's company has quietly overrun the car, killing the guards. Three drunk men shoot up the hill as Maksim and his entourage head down. A stray bullet strikes Angeli between the eyes, and her head jerks back slightly. Valery doesn't see it, but Maksim does, and he immediately changes course.

Maksim sidesteps behind his wife and dives to protect his ten-year-old son as a shotgun charge rips from behind the car and hurls the woman into the air, flying momentarily upward and backward and then to the ground.

When the shooting finally subsided, Maksim wouldn't let his son go to his mother but pulled him away to safety as fast as possible. Maksim and his son escaped unscathed, on the outside at least. But Maksim lost his wife and three men that day, and four suffered injuries.

"You killed her!" Valery had cried bitterly at one point. He was unsure exactly what happened. But he blamed his father for not protecting his mother.

The third and last attack on Maksim was sixteen years ago, three years after Alex and four years after Dmitriy's first vengeful and violent attempt. It marked the tenth anniversary of Maksim's rise to power and his sixtieth birthday. The day Maksim met Alena's mother.

Sitting in his office with Egor, his head of security, Maksim double-checks the arrangements for the big party. People will begin arriving in a few short hours. While reviewing the guest list, an unusual alarm blares in the room and on Maksim's and Egor's phones.

"What's that?" Egor asks.

"Damn. I don't believe it," Maksim says. "Send men to the west wing, now. About ten. But don't leave us vulnerable at the other entrances."

Maxim waits until Egor passes the instructions onto the men, then explains. "It's an alarm that my father had installed ages ago. It's an old tunnel we used for all manner of things. We locked it down but didn't completely seal it off."

"Thankfully, I installed a new wall and door. Because someone's broken through the outer doors."

"Broken through? How far?" Egor asks.

Maksim turns his screen, and Egor bends over the desk to look. While he scrutinizes the floorplan and the men on the monitor as they struggle with the new door, Egor feels Maksim's eyes boring into him, studying him.

Locking eyes with his boss, Egor says, "Do you know them?"

Satisfied with Egor's reaction, Maksim says, "Some of them. The leader, there," and he points. "That's Pavel, Alex's boy," he says, his eyes hard. "And that one, he used to work for Dmitriy. He went into hiding after ... they killed my wife."

Compared to Pavel, who was born into this life, Egor is a relatively new recruit in the business, so he often needs to catch up on some history, but

Maksim sees that mostly as a positive thing.

"Hmmm. What do you want to do with them?"

Maksim reaches for the mouse and presses a red button on the screen. A hissing sound comes from the room, and the seven men begin to panic, but almost immediately, they drop to the floor.

"Check around the house. Round up any others and bring them to that room. Shoot the lot, then burn them. But take Pavel into the room next door. I'll go there and talk with him," Maksim answers coldly.

"Yes, sir," Egor responds without batting an eyelid, then, speaking into his radio, he leaves.

The old mansion has a gigantic, modern combination straw and wood burner installed in an annex at the back of the main building, supposedly to boost the heating in times of extreme cold, of which there are plenty in Belarus. Maksim secretly enhanced the fire, turning it into a monster furnace by adding ferocious gas burners and a processor that grinds any left-over body parts to dust. These additions, usually hidden by a covering of old ash and burnt wood, appear and go into action only when needed. Egor used this crematory on a few occasions during his first year of service for Maksim.

Watching and monitoring while Egor's men carry out their cleanup task, Maksim finally stirs from his chair when Pavel shows signs of recovering. Maksim maintains his video vigil of the scene on a small tablet computer as he walks through the building.

"Do you want me to join you?" Egor asks when Maksim reaches for the door.

Maksim nods as he enters. "Pavel, my young friend. What the hell are you doing here?" Maksim asks the boy in a deceptive, friendly tone and with outstretched arms.

"You murdered my father, you bastard," Pavel spits out. "Your best friend. You killed him!" he yells.

"Yes. And I, too, am still sorry about that. But you must know that he sent Dmitriy against me. And when that failed, he tried to cover it up. After he cocked that up, too, he tried to kill me himself. He would not listen to reason, Pavel. And I can see you won't either," Maksim says, slowly shaking his head and pulling a semi-automatic pistol from his jacket. Then he wastes no further words and shoots the boy between the eyes, just as he shot his father. The bullet exits in a spray of red mist: Pavel's final signs of life.

Jerking his head slightly, Maksim requests Egor to walk with him as he leaves the room. Using hand signals, Egor silently arranges for his men to clean up and lock up again, then he steps briskly alongside his boss as they return to the study.

"From what I hear, that was, fortunately, a lot cleaner than the first attempt," Egor says, daring to mention Alex's previously failed assassination attempt.

But Maksim doesn't respond. Maksim hardly hears Egor as Pavel's words ring in his ears: "You killed him!"

And then his own son's words: *"You killed her! You let them shoot her!"*

Maksim never recovered from the pain of that dreadful moment when they murdered his wife. He still feels it to this day. And sitting in his armchair, mulling over those past events, Maksim realizes it's the first time he's thought about them in years.

It's the whore's death, he thinks. *Making me soft.*

The boy didn't see the first bullet, Maksim remembers. *And he never believed that I'd moved to protect him because she was already lost.* Again, he hears his boy's words. *"You killed her!"* And the bitter tone—and that look.

Maksim recalls seeing that same bitter expression on his son's face only one other time: On the day when Maksim first met the prostitute, Alena's mother. She was a living image of Angeli, Valery's mother, exactly what attracted Maksim to her. But Valery was not impressed and didn't want a new mother.

"Nothing can bring her back," Valery had said, upper lip curled and looking over his shoulder at her. "She's gone, forever," he'd said bitterly.

And Maksim felt the pain of losing her as if it were the day she'd died.

How could I forget whore-day? Valery thinks. *Only four years after Mother's murder, you celebrated the very reason she died!*

Not a day goes by when Valery doesn't think of his mother. Some days, he relives the entire deadly scene with a memory and imagination as vivid as his father's.

Panic struck Valery when the shooting began. Valery was unprepared despite his training and knowledge of the peril accompanying hesitation his father and teachers pounded into him. He'd never experienced real danger before; his father had dealt with all the trouble. This was Valery's first real gunfight.

Valery's head spun, first one way, then the other, and then back again while his mother pulled him down the hill. He couldn't settle on a target as he knew he should. He couldn't decide who to shoot first. Somehow, his hand had found its way into his jacket and was grasping the grip of his small yet powerful pistol, but he couldn't seem to pull it free from its holster.

After what seemed like a thousand shots had passed, his father dives behind his mother just as she lifts into the air. *She's hit!* But Valery doesn't see her after that because his father crashes into him, pulling him to the ground.

All Valery knows is that they shot his mom. And it looked bad. And the earth around them spits out dirt as it sucks up bullets.

"Pull your gun, boy," his father shouts while blasting off a shot. "Pick your target, and shoot!" he says and continues shooting. Valery does as he's told, as he always does.

He first looks in the opposite direction to his father, covering both flanks. Maksim is an excellent marksman, and Valery has inherited his natural skill and cool demeanor. It's easy now that his father has smacked the panic out of him. Aim, shoot, aim, shoot. He picks his targets swiftly, instinctively. Despite his mere ten years of age, he quickly spots the most dangerous assailants, even with peripheral vision. Together, father and son take out eleven men in less than twenty seconds.

Despite their wounds, Maksim's soldiers have taken care of the other attackers and now chase down the two remaining men. Maksim pulls Valery into his arms and carries him screaming, kicking, and punching into the car.

"Mommy! We need to get Mommy!" Valery yells.

But his father pushes the boy into the back seat. A wounded soldier at the wheel rams his foot to the floor, and they speed off, away from the scene and home to safety.

"The men will bring her back," Maksim says. "But she's gone, boy. She's dead, Valery." His words strike like a meteorite dropping from the sky.

A guttural sound forces its way from Valery's throat, as if Valery were looking an enemy in the eye while he cuts the very heart from Valery's living body. Agonizing, watching his heart being dug out, he clenches his teeth and grunts. Not a scream, not "argh," nothing coherent, just a long grunt filled with torment and hatred.

Valery's unsure where to aim his pain-ridden wrath, but ultimately, there is only one choice. So, after quite some time, when he can finally produce discernible words, the boy screams at his father.

"You killed her! You saved me. You saved yourself. But *you let them shoot*

her!" he cries.

Valery's bitter tone cuts into Maksim like a cleaver, and Valery sees his father's pain. He revels in it, grasps it, and slashes himself with its sharp edge as if to ensure it is real, thus causing himself more pain and angering him further. Fury rages like fire within him. *It should have been you who died,* he screams in his mind. "You should have killed me," he wails. And in the corner of the large car seat, he curls up in a ball and embraces the flames consuming his soul.

To this day, Valery maintains his opinion of how his mother died, and he's never forgiven his father. He knows what he saw, despite the explanations—sometimes beaten into him, regardless of seeing his dead mother lying on a slab, a bullet hole in her head.

They wouldn't have killed her if it weren't for his father's life of crime. If Maksim hadn't violently forced his way to the top, his mother would still be alive. Valery was certain.

It's because I blamed him and wouldn't believe him; that's why he got tougher with me, Valery thinks, remembering the last time his father tried to explain what happened.

"No! Liar! She was still standing when you jumped to save me!" Valery remembers shouting.

Then came the blinding pain from the smack that sent him crashing to the floor. Valery had almost choked on his blood. It was only one of many times that his father hit him, but it was by far the hardest, the result of uncontrollable explosive emotion. And the cut on his face stayed open for days afterward.

The vodka is having its way, and Valery feels drowsy. He leans back in the armchair, eyes closed, wallowing in self-pitying memories of his father's ferocious retribution. Valery tries to recall if his father's anger had existed before his mother died, but his thoughts are blurry. Her death overshadows everything.

There is no memory before her death. No life after her death. No life without his mother, without his true love. And no getting her back.

But now there is Alena. She already resembles Mother. My mother. My Alena.

Valery's spirits lift as his idea takes further hold. His thoughts brighten and twist and turn. He shifts ever so slightly in his armchair as if in anticipation.

She *will love me instead. And* she'll *be my wife.* I *will love her and care for her better than* he *ever could. Long after* he *is gone, she'll still be mine. She will be my new love. My new life.*

Maksim observes his son as he stirs on the sofa. He sees the concealed smile growing on Valery's lips at a time when smiles should be few, and he ventures to guess the cause.

"And now Alena is here to forever remind us of her," Maksim says as if stealing thoughts from his son's mind and turning them into words, words better left unspoken.

"*I'll* remember her regardless," Valery says.

Despite the vodka and the late hour, Maksim's guard goes up. "That's good. But you must admit, she does resemble your mother, does she not?"

"Yes, she does. She's a real beauty," Valery says, speaking slowly. But his idea of a future with Alena has a hold on him, like new hope where before there was none. "And *I* will take *good* care of her."

Maksim's brilliant mind stays ever attuned to the minds of others and, in particular, to that which motivates; it's how he's managed to survive and prosper all this time. And he doesn't like what he's hearing. "Of course, you will; she's your sister."

"Yes, of course," Valery says sheepishly.

"So why would you say that?" his father demands, volume rising. Signs of weakness never bode well with Maksim.

"*Because* she is my sister," Valery says, standing, hands on hips. "Because she is *my* sister, and *I* will take care of her. Not like you took care of Mother." Almost shouting now.

"Don't you dare speak of your mother," Maksim shouts, and he stands also. "You treated her like the whore she was. Yet you knew nothing of her or how I cared for her. And don't ever speak of your sister like that. She is not yours!" Maksim yells at his son, raising an open hand to punctuate his words.

"You never took care of her. You hung her out to die!" Valery screams so loud that his voice cracks.

And all the years of Maksim's guilt, despair, pain, and unfair judgmental treatment from his son culminate once more in a hurt-filled, angry explosion. Stepping up to Valery with a deep, loud grunt as he strikes, Maksim smacks his boy with an open palm, just as he did that day—the last time Valery yelled that he'd murdered his mother.

But Valery is thirty now, and he looks like a tank and fights like a Bengal tiger. He doesn't fall, doesn't bleed, doesn't even flinch. Maksim, however, at seventy-six, weakens every day.

"Do *not* hit me ever again," Valery says, punctuating each word, and he swings hard, aiming an uppercut under his father's jaw.

The bigger, older man tries to block with his right, but he's slow, and Valery's prepared a synchronized counter block, smashing down early on Maksim's wrist. At the violent impact of Valery's fist, Maksim's head jerks up, his jaw cracks as it smacks shut, and he crashes backward onto the floor. Maksim doesn't stir, and a moment or two passes before Valery realizes what has happened.

Valery loves his father—in his peculiar fashion. He does not, however, like him. Yet more importantly, Valery respects and fears Maksim and rarely goes against his wishes. But this latest act against him will have consequences, he knows. And Maksim acts more unpredictably with each passing year. Valery can only begin to imagine what his father might do.

How to prepare for the unknown? he thinks, pacing the room. *I don't want to kill him. But I need to create a state* I *control.*

Raising his hand and running it through his hair, he stands still, thinking, and nods a few times. Then, crossing over to his father, Valery checks his breathing, drags him across the floor, and lays him on the sofa. He takes out his phone and calls his private physician while walking away.

"Doc?" he says.

"Yes."

"What are you doing for the next few days? And how would you like to earn some real money?"

Valery's thoughts wander back to Alena while waiting and planning for Doc's arrival. *Beautiful Alena. She'll be all mine,* he thinks again, and an outline of a plan forms in his mind as he prepares to take control of his world. *I'll start with her,* Valery decides, and he calls his documentation specialist.

"I want to see you in my office," Valery says. "Ten, this morning."

A short while later, a staff member shows Doc into the drawing room.

"He fell," Valery says to Doc, waving the girl away.

She takes a sneaky peek at Valery's crotch when turning to leave. Doc pretends not to notice.

"Nasty bump on the head. Can you see how he is?" Valery says, stuffing a heavy roll of one thousand bills into Doc's white coat pocket. "Just for starters. We'll discuss the details later."

After a preliminary check, Doc says, "He appears to be fine. Just obviously

unconscious. I could wake him…"
    "No! I called you here to keep him asleep."

Pillow Talk

Valery pauses, glances back at his father, and then leaves the bedroom, entrusting Doc with Maksim's care. Walking along the corridor, Valery writes a message to Boris on his phone: Drawing room Meet ASAP Confidential.

Boris's response arrives fast: 15 mins.

On the heavy wooden table beside his armchair, Valery's glass is still half full. He sits, drinks, and lets his mind drift, mulling over the fight with Maksim earlier. His father's comment about Valery treating his mother like a whore tugs at his conscience.

He knew, Valery thinks, closing his eyes, and almost unbidden, he sees a memory he rarely permits.

"Hurry, Sweetie, before anyone sees us," Angeli says, rushing Valery along the corridor. She stops, opens a door, and ushers him through.

Oh, it's big, Valery thinks, standing just inside the room. He looks around almost reverently. *I shouldn't be here.*

Angeli turns the key in the lock and goes to inspect the faint bruise on Valery's face. "He was hard on you today, I see."

Valery shrugs. "It's OK." But at the mention of his father, he glances at the door.

"No, it's not OK. And don't worry, Val. It's quite safe. He won't be home until tomorrow afternoon," Angeli says.

She leads Valery by the hand and sits him on the edge of the bed. Kneeling in front of him, she cups his face in her hands.

"I wish I could take you away from here," she says. "But I can't …"

"Yes, you could! You could rescue me from … this!" he says, pointing at his face. "And I could take care of you."

"No, Valery," Angeli says, shaking her head. "He'd find us. And God only knows what he would do. The best I can do is protect your heart."

Valery stares at the floor between his feet.

After a moment, she asks him, "Have you ever kissed a girl?"

The boy looks up into her eyes and shakes his head. "I don't want a girl. I only need you."

Angeli attempts to smile, but her lips turn down, and she sighs. "If only I'd met *you* when I was younger."

She tilts his head back to one side, leans forward, and kisses him gently. Using her thumb, she pries his lower lip open while pressing down gently on his chin.

Should I kiss her back? How *do I kiss her?* Valery thinks.

Taking his upper lip between hers, Angeli tugs a little, waiting for him to respond. When he does, she pulls back and stands, then strokes his cheek.

"You must never tell anyone that you've been here. Tata will kill you if he finds out you've been with his woman. Even if it's only rumors."

"Yes, Mama."

"This evening, Val, we are alone. And I am yours, and you are mine. So, call me Angeli," she says as she turns her back to him. "Undo my dress, will you?"

Valery stands, tall for his age, and his mother is only a little above average height. He easily reaches up to grasp the zipper and pulls it down, revealing and staring at the bare skin of her back.

Angeli faces him and slides the dress slowly off her shoulders, letting it drop to the floor. Then, spreading her arms out a little, she presents herself to him dressed only in an almost-see-through bra and panties. She steps forward, close to him.

The boy glances down, but by pressing her fingers under his chin, Angeli makes him look up at her. His face brushes against her breasts through the almost invisible nylon.

Valery breathes in deeply.

I can almost taste her.

Angeli rubs herself against his lips and says, "I'd like to shower. Will you come with me and wash my back?"

Valery nods.

"Help me with these, will you?" she says.

Taking one of his hands, she slides it under her bra strap and nudges his fingers off the edge of her shoulder, pulling the thin line of elastic with them. Then down, revealing her breast.

Valery holds his breath.

Her skin feels soft under his touch, and his fingertips tingle. Valery becomes more confused and flustered with each stitch they remove together.

His face flushes bright red.

Valery studies every inch of her as she guides his hands to places they should not be. Unwittingly, he falls deeper and deeper into young love's trap.

Naked, beautiful, looking like a goddess, she peels off his clothes, sliding her caressing fingers all over his body. The hairs on his neck and arms raise to her touch. His nerves chill through him to that tantalizing, body-twisting place in the small of his back as her hand drifts down his spine, teasing, tickling.

Finally, Angeli takes Valery toward the bathroom and the shower. The child goes in, a young boy. A lifetime later, he emerges as a man, besotted, proud, and in awe. Born again, saved by true love, he climbs into bed beside his very own divine angel.

Rescued anyway, he thinks, lying back and smiling.

Valery wakes before Angeli the next morning. He turns onto his side and stares at her lying naked beside him, the sheet covering only her hips and legs. *She loves me more than she loves him because I am from her body,* he thinks. Reaching out a hand, he gently glides his knuckles down her breast, over her nipple, like she taught him the previous evening.

Angeli opens her eyes.

"Will you marry me?" Valery says. He holds his breath, waiting. He's sure that only minutes ago, he was dreaming about this moment, and this question, but he can't quite remember. Nevertheless, he's certain that in his dreams, she says yes.

"Oh, Valery," Angeli says, laughing, her smile radiant.

The boy feels his heart pounding against the inside of his chest.

"Don't ever say something like that in front of your father," his mother says. "That *would* get me killed."

"No! I will protect you," Valery says and frowns. *I will marry you one day. You'll see!*

Angeli smiles, shakes her head, and strokes his cheek. "Milashka, if you promise me to keep these thoughts to yourself, then yes, I will marry you someday."

"I promise!" Valery says, and his smile lights up his whole face like a newborn star saving a far-off world from an eternity of darkness.

The following day, while Valery dresses himself for their annual visit to his dead grandfather's grave, his mother comes bursting into his room.

"You left a sock under the bed the other evening," she says. "If your father asks you anything, then you must lie convincingly! You were not in our room. Understand?"

Is that why he let her die?

A loud knocking sound causes Valery to stir. He folds his arms across his chest, instinctively sliding his primary shooting hand inside his jacket. The drawing room door opens, then loudly closes moments later. Valery opens his eyes.

"You sent for me, sir?" Boris says.

"My father is in a coma, it seems. He fell and hit his head."

"I'm sorry to hear that," Boris says.

"Yes ... well. It's not sure how long he will remain in that condition. So, I'll be running things for a while."

"Yes, sir."

"I don't know what *you* think, but I believe that security in this place has been shot to hell these past few years."

"I couldn't agree more, sir," Boris says, his gaze cold and unflinching.

Valery nods slowly, a few times, eyes locked on Boris's, his expression hardening as a frown forms. "It's time to correct that. I'm sure your boss is to blame, and I intend to deal with him. But I would appreciate your help—if you want to stand with me?"

Boris's gaze softens marginally. "Of course, sir."

"Then let's do it now before the news is out, and we lose the element of surprise."

LYRA

One of the most painful periods of Maksim's life that he could remember to date was when he was dealing with his grief after his wife's death and the unexpected responsibility of raising a ten-year-old child alone. Valery's trauma of losing his mother only made the whole situation worse.

One hundred and twenty years ago—four years after Valery's mother dies

Experts recommend various mechanisms for handling grief, ranging from ensuring a system of regular support, like meeting a family member, friend, or psychologist, to the insane ideas of writing a letter to the dead or celebrating a deceased relative's birthday. Being no specialist in all this psychical crap, Maksim researched this advice in magazines, library books, and some online. And he's tried many approaches. Not himself, of course. And no bloody anniversary of her death, no, no. He hired help, and a host of new trainers in new skills to keep the boy's mind occupied.

For the most part, however, Maksim avoided directly tackling the emotional subjects. He achieved this by simply disagreeing with much of the psycho-horseshit he read about. At some point, he brought in two psychologists to help assess Valery's emotional state. He told them everything he felt was relevant to Valery's case. His mother's violent death story. That he, Maksim, was, out of necessity, hard on the boy during training and how his mother used to compensate, and so, how close Valery became to his mother. A little too much, Maksim had divulged. Never once, though, did he mention the sock under the bed.

But when Valery—despite his young age—kicked each counselor out in succession, screaming and shouting that he will never forget his mother and that nothing will replace her and that he would stick their fucking textbooks where the sun don't shine if they ever showed their faces again, Maksim decided that emotionally, the boy was fine. *Don't want him becoming soft anyway,* he thought.

Nevertheless, despite the relatively successful outcome of Valery's mental assessment and all Maksim's other attempts to distract the boy, Valery wasn't responding. He did his chores, his schoolwork, and his training. But otherwise, he kept himself to himself and hardly spoke at all.

Maksim had watched—to his mind—the boy changing over the years. He imagined something ugly growing inside, like an invisible, deadly fungus that spread in a thick microscopic layer, a mutating, multiplying sickness waiting to pounce and explode all over the boy, devouring the son he once knew.

Sometimes, Maksim would tiptoe past Valery's bedroom door. He would stand and listen as Valery cried himself to sleep. And he was sure the boy did that every night. But he'd never been there by chance when Valery masturbated in bed.

So, Maksim neither heard the boy's whispered cusses and threats. "You left me! You selfish bitch! You left me alone with him. So now you'll suffer like you made me suffer." Yanking so hard, it must have hurt.

Nor the aftermath, crying into his pillow. "I'm sorry, Mama. I didn't mean to hurt you. Please don't go. *Please come back!*"

Maybe things would have turned out differently if Maksim had heard all that. But he didn't, and now, he's out of options, it seems. Stubborn as ever, though, he doesn't want to give up. So, he does what he's been avoiding all this time. He calls Doc.

"Thank you for coming, Doc. I'm sure you're a busy man," Maksim says, pouring vodka.

They raise their glasses. They drink, then sit.

"I need some advice."

"Valery?"

It wasn't hard to guess. Valery's the only reason Maksim ever called Doc in previously.

Maksim nods. "I simply don't know what to do anymore. It's been years already, and I've tried all the textbook stuff. It's like he's completely lost."

"You do know chemistry's my thing, not emotions?"

Maksim huffs and flicks back his head.

"But tell me, what have you tried so far?"

For an hour or two, they sit, drink vodka, and talk. Maksim explains. Doc listens, prompts, and questions until Maksim runs out of words.

"He needs to find something to fill the emptiness," Doc says. "Something or someone that grabs him. Snags him. Consumes him, almost. ... I know it sounds absurd, but what about a dog?"

"Are you seriously comparing a mother to a dog?"

"No, of course not. But it might help pull him out of his depression. Probably best not to make your motive obvious, though. Maybe make it part of his training. Security, or something."

Maksim rubs his chin, his eyes chasing his thoughts around the room. "He does enjoy training and playing with the other dogs. ... You know, I think that might work. At least to get the boy started. Then we'll see where to go from there." *And it might even allow me to get closer to him.* Maksim personally trains all his guard dogs, and the boy knows that.

Maksim sits behind his computer and starts researching the dogs offered by his usual kennels and breeders. "Come. Come," he says, beckoning Doc over.

After a few moments, Maksim points. "Look at that. Two litters. The largest kennel around here. Perfect!"

"They look cute."

"Doc, you're invited to dinner. This evening," Maksim says, as close to excitement as he ever comes. "I think it should be you who mentions the idea. Valery ... has taken to rejecting most of my suggestions."

Doc bows his head ever so slightly. "But under no circumstances should he know we planned this."

What's he *doing here?* Valery thinks as he enters the dining room.

Drinking a whisky aperitif, Doc and Maksim sit talking, waiting for Valery to join them. "It's been a long time since we've had any guests for dinner, Valery," Maksim says. "And I think it's time to change that. So, I've started with Doc. A friendly, familiar face will help to get us going again."

Valery recalls the last time his father tried to hold a dinner party. *Three weeks after Mother's death!* It ended in a public slap to his face and Maksim sending him to his room.

While Maksim explains the visitor's presence, Doc stands, and Valery walks over to him. They shake hands like adults. Valery glances over the man's head at his father, who's watching his every move, as usual.

"My, you've grown! It's good to see you, Valery. It's been a long time. I hear your father has laid out a grueling education program for you," Doc says.

"He keeps me busy," Valery says, pursing his lips and forcing a straight-lined smile. Then he inclines his head slightly, circles around Doc, and heads for the place set for him beside his father.

Doc humphs, smiles, and sits back down. "A long time, indeed," he says quietly to himself.

"Whisky?" Maksim says, looking at his son.

Valery raises his eyebrows.

"Oh, come on. I know you're drinking the stuff."

Valery's cheeks take on a mild pink hue, but he doesn't hesitate to look at the butler standing on the opposite side of the room. *It's about time,* he thinks, clenches his jaw, then nods a curt yes, like any man would.

"And talking of spirits, we should soon invite Gorelik, the distillery owner, and his family. Word has it that he's created a special new vodka blend, and I'd like to try it. Don't you go to school with Natallia, his daughter, Valery?"

Valery nods.

"She must be about your age. Is she in your class?"

"One year above me."

"Hmmm. Pretty girl. And blonde. I've always had a soft spot for blondes but could never snag one. And already, the last time I saw her, it looked like she was pretty well stacked. You must have noticed that, Val?"

"I'm not interested. And please call me Valery."

"I don't know. When I was a lad your age, they'd accuse you of being gay if you hadn't already announced—in style—the loss of your virginity," Maksim said.

"Oh, he has some time yet, Maksim. Not all boys jump into a girl's panties the moment they grow hair on their balls," Doc says.

Valery snorts a laugh and grins.

"I noticed you were out with the dogs earlier," Doc says, looking at Valery.

"I take one of them running with me every day."

"Ah, that sounds nice. I've always wanted one myself. So, who gets tired first—you or the dog?"

"Me, every time," Valery says, chuckling. "Why don't you get one?"

"It's a long story. Which one is yours?"

"They all belong to Father."

"Yes, they do," Maksim says. "And now you mention dogs, I'm one down. I'm going to a kennel tomorrow to pick a new one."

"Interesting," Doc says. "How old?"

"The litter was born a week ago."

"Can you take them home that young?" Doc asks Valery.

"I don't know."

"No, no. At eight to nine weeks old. Here," Maksim says, and he reaches inside his jacket, pulls out some papers, and hands them to Doc. "Look at those. They don't even have their eyes open yet."

The inkjet-printed pictures are not top-quality glossies but plenty good enough to see the closed eyes and shiny pelts.

"Cute," Doc says after studying the photos, then he reaches out to hand them back to Maksim.

"May I see?" Valery asks.

"I can't imagine why not," Doc says and hands the papers to him.

Maksim and Doc watch the boy as he studies the images.

"You know, I would be interested in going along with you. For the experience," Doc says.

"You're more than welcome," Maksim says.

Valery doesn't exactly smile as he gazes at those suckling bundles of silky dark hair, but his eyes light up, and it could seem as if he were trying to avoid giveaway signs of affection while greeting a secret lover. Even through paper and ink, the tiny creatures were conjuring their puppy magic.

"May I come too?" he says.

After that evening at dinner, Maksim's and Doc's plan gets easier at each turn or each trip to the kennel. All the puppy cuteness clearly enamors Valery. They agree to go and see the black and brown babes once a week, and Maksim reserves the first choice of the litter until week six. But already during the third visit, Valery's unable to contain himself.

"I like this one. Can I have her, Father?"

Maksim feigns surprise. "A girl?"

"I've been watching, Valery. And I think she's a good choice," Doc says. "Because she obviously likes you. But if you take one, Valery, you should have her as your own. Not to live with the other dogs, but with you. You don't need a guard dog at your age. If you ask me, she should just be a pet."

"You'll still need to get her spayed," Maksim says.

"When does that happen?" Doc asks.

"I always do it after the first full cycle," Maksim answers. "Gives them a chance to mature."

"Can she sleep in my room?" Valery says, looking at his father.

Maksim nods. "If you choose a girl, you could even call her Angeli in memory of your mother," he says thoughtfully.

A bloody dog won't bring her back! Valery thinks. *Nor replace her!* He scowls.

Doc chips in. "I always find that animals' names are much easier when they're only one or two syllables. Your other dogs have astronomical names, don't they?"

"Correct," Maksim says.

The girl puppy licks Valery's face, and he smiles.

"It might be an idea to stick with that theme," Doc says. "There are enough short names to choose from, yet not too many."

"I've already chosen," Valery says. "She'll be called Lyra."

Doc inclines his head respectfully. "You know your astronomy, I see. The northern constellation that holds ... which star?"

"Vega," Valery says and smiles. "It's Lyra's brightest star."

And so, it was settled.

Lyra jumps up with her forepaws on Valery's chest, and he laughs out loud for the first time in years as he lies back and lets the dog lick his face.

It seems to Maksim that the only problem remaining is that eight weeks have not yet passed, but Lyra and Valery have already sealed their bond.

Lyra grows fast, transforming quickly into a strong, fit young animal that easily outruns her companion. Valery lets Maksim help him train Lyra—through formal instruction sessions mostly because Maksim takes his dogs seriously.

"Never let them get the upper hand," Maksim repeats continuously. "Watch for the low growl. If that happens, find a way to deflate the situation. But don't run, and don't enter the conflict. Ever!" he warns. And when training with the guard dogs: "Never bring Lyra in here when all the dogs are loose. That could go very wrong," he says over and over until Valery finally blurts out, "OK, I got it! I got it."

Valery knows his father wants to get more out of the training sessions, and he tries to open up to Maksim. But he also instinctively keeps a distance, guessing that his father is using the dog to get closer to him. And Valery has still not forgiven Maksim for letting his mother die. *And I never will.*

Maksim doesn't push too hard; he settles for what he can get. *Things are at least getting better.* But he still tiptoes up to the bedroom door during the first year to listen. Valery's crying doesn't last as long as before, and Maksim imagines Lyra licking the tears from the boy's face. *It might go faster if that bloody photo wasn't beside his bed,* Maksim thinks.

It took years for Valery to make his next move, if one could call it a move. By chance, or maybe by fate, Valery followed Natallia to the same college after secondary school, and he'd been watching her.

He smiled at her across the canteen one day when lunch was over, and she was clearing away her food. Natallia made a point of hanging back, waiting for him to return his food tray.

"Your dog is quite beautiful," she says as he approaches her. "What's her name?"

"Lyra. It's a northern constellation that holds ..."

"Vega," she says.

He smiles.

"Can I meet her? Is she safe? Will she eat me up?"

"No, *she* won't. But ..." *I might.* Valery smiles. His face flushes light red.

"Well, she's quite safe. Come to my car after class."

"I will," Natallia says, smirking.

Later, by the car, Lyra jumps up and licks the girl all over, so much she almost falls.

"Lyra, heel." The dog obeys.

"I'd love to go for a walk with her," Natallia says. "You can come too if you like." She smiles, a cheeky, taunting glint in her eyes.

"Lyra and I go every day. So, sure. Whenever you like."

The next day, the sun hangs halfway in the blue western sky, blazing constantly, covered only momentarily and from time to time by passing white bundles of fluff. Lying on their backs in the grass, Valery and Natallia watch the clouds float after each other, pushed onward by a lazy breeze. Lyra prances like a gazelle, then goes down on her front haunches, barking quietly, a twist of excitement coloring her voice.

"Go chase a rabbit or something," Valery says.

Natallia chuckles, turns on her side, props herself up on one elbow, and looks at him. "I've never seen you with any other girls at school," she says.

"Correct."

"Why not?"

He turns his head sideways and looks at her. "I'm very busy out of school. I don't have time."

"Not even one girlfriend?"

"No."

"I'm sure you could make time. If you wanted."

He pauses a long time before answering. "I'm ... not used to it," he says, looking at the clouds again.

"Used to what?"

Again, he makes her wait. "Being around girls. Talking with them."

"You just need practice," Natallia says, lying back on the grass again.

As if it were that simple. Valery turns his head and studies her. *She's quite gorgeous,* he thinks. *And he's right. She does have a nice pair.*

One year later

Valery wakes up and turns to look at Natallia, but Lyra licks his face. He laughs and rises up to lean on his elbow.

Valery reaches over the dog, says, "Hi," and strokes Natallia's face. He slides his hands down her neck to her naked breasts and squeezes gently. "Let's get this dog out of here."

"No, Valery, we'll be late for school. And I have extra math on Friday." Her expression is cold and unfriendly, as if she'd woken up angry.

"You can miss it once. You hate it anyway."

"Exactly why I'm no good at it. But I need it, and I need to be there," she says.

"I thought you *were* good at it?"

"Well, not good enough." She looks away.

That's not true, he thinks. *And it's not the first time she's said no. Like she's punishing me.*

"Lyra, down!" Valery says, then moves over beside Natallia. "What's wrong?" He strokes her face.

She hesitates, but then blurts it out. "What's wrong? You don't know?"

Valery shakes his head.

"You hurt me last night. And you're doing it more and more these past months. And I don't understand it or like it."

"Oh, Sweetie, I'm sorry. I had a bit too much to drink last night. And I guess I still don't know my own strength. You should have told me I was hurting you."

"I tried. But you just said sorry and then continued. Look at this," Natallia says, showing him the bruises high on her shoulders, close to the base of her neck. Small bruises, but they shouldn't even be there.

"Oh, no. I'm so sorry," Valery says, gently kissing the blue patches on her skin. "Let me make it up to you. I'm sure I can bring a smile to your face before we leave this bed."

"Maybe you could, but I don't feel like it. I'm hurting right now, inside and out."

"Inside?"

"My feelings," she says, and pulls away and leaves the bed.

Maksim walks in on Valery and Natallia while they're at the breakfast table. "That bacon smells good!

"I hope you've remembered Doc is coming to dinner this evening. And he'll be staying the weekend. It's been a while, and we have things to discuss. And he really wants to meet this blonde beauty that's competing for your time, Valery."

"We've remembered. But I really think it's wishful thinking of you to call it a competition," Natallia says, smiling.

Maksim throws back his head and snorts.

After the greeting and during aperitifs in the drawing room, the butler enters, coughs lightly, and announces dinner. Lyra follows Valery and Natallia as they trail the others into the dining room.

Maksim looks back at them and says, "I've told you before, you're not to have that mutt in here when we have g …"

"Yes, I know, you say that every time, Father. But Natallia isn't a guest, and Doc is an old friend."

"Don't mind me," Doc says as he takes his place close to Maksim at the table's end and winks at Valery.

Natallia sits opposite him in Valery's usual place, Valery on her far side.

Doc continues. "I believe it was my advice to have her as a pet and to keep her at your side every moment you could, wasn't it?"

"Hmmm. I don't remember those exact words," Maksim says. But he chuckles, then indicates to the staff to begin serving dinner.

Valery looks at the butler as he serves Valery's food, jerks his head slightly, twice, and the servant responds with two extra slabs of meat. A little later, when he thinks no one is looking, piece by piece, Valery slips the steaks to Lyra and smiles warmly as she gulps it down.

Barely holding back his smile, Maksim glances at Doc and nods.

"What a wonderful idea it was to get Lyra," Doc says.

"Except for the rocketed cost of steak consumption ever since," Maksim complains, and everyone laughs.

Valery's thoughts vaguely wander to the past—more by reaction than choice—as his mind assesses something he can't quite place. It's not happiness. That's out of the question without …. But it feels as if these past few years have been the best since …. But then Maksim interrupts his thoughts.

"It's your birthday in a few months, Valery. And it's a big one. Do you have any idea how you want to celebrate it?"

"Not at all."

"Maybe Natallia can help you. She must have been through a million options preparing her eighteenth last year."

"I think it was possibly quite different for Natallia than it is for Valery," Doc says.

Natallia raises her eyebrows and nods three times, big, exaggerated movements.

"Not that you couldn't help, my dear."

And so, Doc and Natallia hit it off like a house on fire. He can be friendly and companionable and someone you can warm to despite his dry, sarcastic humor, and as long as you don't know what he does for a living. And his hobbies are worse. As for Natallia, everyone loves her wit, looks, and dazzling laugh and smile. And this evening, for some reason, she shines and entertains more than ever.

Maybe it was the conversation running away with her that caused her not to notice that she was also drinking more than ever. Perhaps it was Doc's white powder that Valery had secretly shared by spiking her drinks. Either way, much later, well after the house staff have withdrawn, Valery lifts Natallia up from a sofa and carries her to the bedroom. And he does his utmost to avoid any more bruises.

Valery always wakes early, and the next morning is no exception. He sneaks out of bed, leaving Natallia sleeping off her excess alcohol. *At least I can take a decent walk this morning,* he thinks, dressing quietly and quickly. On the days Natallia sleeps over, pre-breakfast activities usually cut out quite a chunk of the morning, meaning a much shorter walk with Lyra, which always annoys Valery despite the reason.

Downstairs, with Lyra patiently waiting beside him, Valery ties up his walking boots' thick laces, straps his hunting knife on his belt, and hurriedly dons a thin summer vest—the only outdoor garment hanging readily available. *It will have to do,* he thinks. Lyra prances and yaps as Valery chooses a ball from a cupboard drawer beside the shoe rack.

Without so much as a coffee or a vodka to kickstart the day, Valery marches out toward the dog pen where the guard dogs live, some sixty meters or so from the house. He usually takes one or two dogs walking with them. Lyra barks and jumps in the air, looking at the pocket where Valery's hand holds the ball.

He's early this morning, Maksim thinks, looking out his study window. He watches as Valery throws the ball, well to the left of the dogs' area. *Just like I taught him.* "Don't get them excited, don't get their competitive spirits up. Let sleeping dogs lie, so to speak," Maksim had said countless times.

Maksim humphs and smiles, then turns back to Doc, who's also watching Valery and Lyra. "I guess Sleeping Beauty's still unconscious," Maksim says and chuckles.

"You pushed her too hard. She couldn't keep up," Doc replies.

"I didn't pour it down her throat," Maksim says, half smiling, half frowning.

Lyra holds the ball out for Valery. He takes it from between her teeth and throws it again.

"Now, Doc, tell me about this new drug," Maksim says.

"I beg your pardon?"

"Ah, yes. Your father told m ..."

"He shouldn't have done that! It's secret."

"But your father and I go way back. And ..."

"Nevertheless, he shouldn't have told anyone. It's *my* secret."

"Doesn't your father pay all the bills?" Maksim's tone is low and cold. "He employs you, doesn't he? Which means technically, it's *his* secret." Maksim was prepared. Doc's father had helped him with that. And with a routine of going abroad often, he'd also ensured he was away this weekend—to avoid this very conversation.

Doc sighs. He knows it's no use arguing with Maksim.

Still playing ball, Lyra and Valery come gradually closer to the other dogs. This time, Lyra runs ahead, anticipating the throw. Valery chucks the ball again, carefully aiming for the dog because she's not far from the double row of metal fence.

"How long do you expect it to take?" Maksim says.

Lyra jumps to catch but misses, and the ball smacks hard against her upper jaw and bounces in a sharp arc high into the air. It lands between the outer and inner guard dogs' fence, closer to the dogs' side than the surrounding garden. Lyra paws at it but can't reach. The other dogs look on from a distance.

Shit, Valery thinks, then shivers. Despite the frequently warm second-summer afternoons, the early morning temperature is lower than he was used to when summer was at its best, now that late autumn rushes to make up for lost time.

Valery makes a split-second decision. *Need to get that ball before there's trouble,* he thinks.

After a long pause, Doc says, "Hard to guess. It could take a year ..."

Valery opens the gate to the dog pen. Lyra follows. Ignoring his father's many warnings, Valery lets her in but keeps her close. "Lyra, heel!"

"Never let her in there alone. And never go in there when all the dogs are loose together." Maksim had warned him often. But that was long ago when Valery was still learning. Now he knows what he's doing.

And Valery knows that all but two night-duty dogs will be loose in the pen this early. But now, he can only see three. Sol, an alpha male known for his hot temper; Jupiter, another alpha, named because of his size; and Luna, the sweetest of the pack and Sol's favorite, named after her cool temperament. *The others must be sleeping,* he thinks. *It'll be OK for a minute or so.*

"... Or it could take five," Doc continues. "And there's always the risk it might lead to nothing."

Once Valery closes the outside gate, he opens the second metal door, and dog and master enter the enclosure.

"Sol, Jupiter, Luna, down!" Valery commands. "Lyra, down."

After a moment's thought, Maksim says, "Why so long? And why the uncertainty? I thought the base drugs were commonplace?"

"Well ..." Doc begins.

Valery steps briskly over to the fence and retrieves the ball. Sol could have easily grabbed it with his teeth if he'd wanted. But he doesn't play much.

Valery shivers again. *Damn. It's too cold to go walking dressed like this,* he realizes, stuffing the ball into his vest pocket. He studies the other dogs for a moment. "Sol, here," he says, and the dog comes to him.

"Lyra," Valery says, holding out his palm.

Sol turns to his side as Lyra stands. He licks her face.

They'll be fine while I grab a coat, Valery thinks, and he turns toward the gate. "Lyra, stay."

To avoid his father's gaze, Valery runs through the garden, staying behind the line of bushes separating the grass from the flower beds. He heads back down the path leading to the back entrance hall and cloakroom. When he reaches the open spot where he knows his father can see him, he crosses his arms around his chest, hugging himself and rubbing his arms briskly up and down.

Maksim does indeed notice Valery hurrying down the pathway and vaguely registers him rubbing his arms in his T-shirt and vest and ignores the unbidden thought: *Idiot.* He turns his attention back to Doc's captivating explanation of how mixing powerful drugs can have devastating effects. Even deadly.

As Valery rushes through the backdoor, he's too far away to hear the low growl deep in Luna's throat. He certainly can't see her upper lips quivering ever so slightly as she watches Sol with Lyra.

Nobody knows Luna has come in heat for the first time, except for her. And the other dogs.

Valery rushes to the cloakroom, grabs his lined leather jacket, and returns outside in less than fifteen seconds. Struggling to pull on his coat as he runs up the path, he reaches the grass just in time to hear Luna's first low bark. Not loud. Not yet. A warning.

Doc has finished talking for now. Maksim stares at the dark wood of his office bureau, frowning, his mind searching for something that's bothering him. Then, he realizes.

He didn't see Lyra coming back to the house with Valery.

Valery calls out as he runs across the grass. "Luna, down!" But she doesn't respond. With head lowered slightly and gaze focused on Lyra, she growls openly and loudly. Showing her bright white fangs from under raised and quivering upper lips, she continues advancing.

Lyra begins growling as she slowly backs up toward the entrance gate. Sol looks on as if trying to decide what to do.

Maksim stands and looks out the window. He sees Valery rushing to the first gate, then he looks for the dogs.

Luna barks once. A snarling, vicious, teeth-baring bark.

Maksim rushes to open the window. "Don't go in there!" he yells.

Valery pushes open the first gate. The automatic locking system makes him wait for the gate to click back into place before he can start on the second. He pushes against the metal bars, forcing the mechanism to close faster.

Still retreating backward, Lyra is almost level with Valery on the other side of the fence. Sol starts growling at Luna. And Jupiter, the largest and strongest of all the dogs but not the brightest, sticks his nose in the air and sniffs in the direction of Luna's enticing rear end.

Need to get Lyra out, Valery thinks.

Maksim, cold and angry, cool and collected, jerks open a drawer on the right side of his bureau. He grabs his Walter PK380. He keeps the laser attached, ready for quick yet precision shooting.

Even at sixty-three and despite his incredible size, Maksim is quick and nimble on his feet. He skirts around the desk; yanks open the door and dashes out. Doc follows at a more cautious pace.

The other dogs appear from left and right, gathering to see what all the noise is about. Saturn—another alpha male—and his good-looking Venus form the third pair of the group. The two underdogs, Mars and Neptune, trail them. Carina, the oldest of the group and Jupiter's favorite girl, comes up last, still a little sleepy but waking up fast.

Valery starts pushing open the second gate. It's heavy. Lyra hears the latch and feels the metal bars pressing against her rump. Valery's trying to open the gate without trapping Lyra's paws under it and compromising her position. Lyra turns to look at Valery.

Something sparks Luna's anger a notch beyond her control. No one will ever know what it was. Dogs in heat can be unpredictable and uncharacteristically aggressive. Maybe it was only that. Or perhaps it was Lyra looking away. Maybe she felt Jupiter's nose against her as he sniffed her.

With a ferocious growl and a wildness in her glare, Luna takes her chance and snaps at Lyra's mouth, just as Jupiter licks Luna from behind.

Lyra yelps as Luna's teeth cut the surface of the soft flesh of her lips as she jumps backward, smashing harder against the gate, which slams against Valery as he squirms inside. The gate's frame bashes against his left wrist, trapping it between the metal door posts. He screams in agony, Lyra's weight pressing him hard against the fence.

Even before Luna completes her first lunge at Lyra, she twists her head and shoulders, doubling backward to see what's attacking her from behind. She snaps at Jupiter; he growls and barks back. Sol snarls at Jupiter and Luna, trying to keep them both in check.

Ignoring the pain in his left wrist, pushing against Lyra with his knees, and pulling the gate open with one hand, Valery yanks himself free. With his undamaged right hand, he searches under his jacket for his hunting knife.

Lyra doesn't hesitate to take advantage of Luna's distraction, and she bites Luna square in the neck, high up and close to Luna's throat. And she doesn't let go. Luna's howls of agony signify the first serious injury of the fight.

Sol snarls and snaps at Lyra and bites the side of her face and ear. But she still doesn't release her grip on Luna.

Raising his knife hand high, Valery slams his arm down, aiming for Sol's shoulder, but Jupiter attacks Sol from behind for some reason. Crunching Sol's back leg between his strong fangs, Jupiter's huge teeth easily crush the bone. The cracking sound would be audible if not for all the snarling, barking, and growling.

Sol lets go of Lyra and howls; Lyra releases Luna and whirls around to bite Sol, but Sol's body drops toward the ground as Jupiter pulls on his broken leg. Lyra's mouth misses Sol and passes directly under Valery's knife as he slashes downward, aiming initially at Sol.

The sharp blade slices through Lyra's upper mouth and carves the lip clean off, revealing her jaw and jagged white teeth. Arm in full swing, there's no stopping the knife as it continues to cut through Lyra's lower lip and mouth. Half the lower lip hangs loose, and Lyra's bright red blood splatters all over Valery's face and jacket as Lyra tries to shake off the attack.

In a frenzy, Lyra lunges and snaps at the closest enemy she can find. Valery. She clamps his already damaged left wrist in her jaw and bites. But even before Valery's mind registers the pain, he sees a red dot appear between Lyra's eyes.

BANG!

Lyra's head jerks back as Maksim's custom-made bullet blows holes through the front and out the base of her skull. Valery's anguished heart explodes, and he instantly wishes the bullet had gone through him.

BANG! Maksim's next headshot cleanly takes out Jupiter.

Sol and Luna both lie on the ground. Luna's breathing is labored; the dark red, sticky blood soaking through her neck's thick fur has long stopped pouring out. Unable to stand, Sol whimpers as he licks at Luna's wounds.

BANG! With a rock-hard expression, yet eyes screwed up, Maksim shoots his favorite, Sol. Doc flinches when the gun explodes. Valery, too, but he doesn't show it.

BANG! Bye-bye, sweet Luna.

Up in the bedroom, youth conquers the mistreatment Natallia's body suffered the night before. Despite her condition, the far-off explosions from Maksim's pistol cause her to stir and awaken. She crawls out of bed and cradles her sensitive head while walking to the window.

Natallia has to study the scene in the dog pen below for some time before understanding what she sees. *Oh, my God!* Then she rushes to pull on some clothes.

Valery falls to his knees, then flat on his shins. Leaning forward, he grabs Lyra's forelegs and pulls her to him, onto his lap, ignoring the blood staining his clothes. Withdrawn and silent, he presses his cheek against Lyra's ruined, bloody face and rocks a few times back and forth.

"Kennel!" Maksim says, closer by now, and he escorts the remaining dogs inside and locks them up. On returning to Valery's side, with a stone-cold look, he says, "Furnace," as if one-word sentences might prevent him from releasing a torrent of words and emotions. Who knows what's churning inside that giant human cauldron, but none of it's good; that's almost certain.

Valery doesn't respond verbally, but he also doesn't wait, as if he doesn't want to delay the obvious and doesn't want to stay with his father to face the music. With a harsh look on his face, he lovingly picks up his beloved, dead companion in his arms, and with Doc's help, he negotiates the gates and walks through the garden. He heads for the outside door to the furnace room.

Natallia meets Valery at the edge of the grass. She's already crying when she stands before him, making him stop. She doesn't notice his jaw clenching tighter.

"I'm so sorry," she says.

Valery steps around Natallia and continues on his way. Natallia follows. Valery doesn't say a word.

Natallia stays with him when he cremates Lyra in the furnace. She stays with him all day.

Valery doesn't speak all day, even when Doc comes to tend to his wounds.

Natallia tries talking with Valery. Valery doesn't respond. He rocks backward and forward a lot.

They don't go down for dinner. Vodka. They drink a lot of vodka and beer.

At the dinner table, Maksim says to Doc, "If he wasn't my son, I'd kill him myself."

Natallia persuades Valery to go to bed early. She's rather drunk and has got it into her head that she can bring Valery out of his depression with sex.

After a few moments, however, Natallia cries out. "No, Valery. Stop! Stop! You're hurting me!"

Valery slaps her so hard that he cracks her delicate jaw, and then he continues to pump all his anger into her.

Natallia screams and cries.

"You killed her!" Valery shouts at one point.

"Stop, stop." Natallia whimpers and cries some more.

A little later, *"You left me!"* he yells.

Natallia cries and cries and cries until she has nothing left, until finally, Valery rolls off her, exhausted. She crawls quietly out of bed and grabs a dressing gown as she crosses the room. She goes down to the drawing room and falls in through the door.

Doc immediately runs to help Natallia. He sends the house staff to retrieve his medical bag from the guest bedroom.

On seeing the girl's state, Maksim's emotions win over his self-control, and he storms off to find his son.

Valery's wounds take almost two weeks to heal to a level where he can show his face in public. No one kills Maksim's dogs and gets away with it lightly.

In the meantime, Doc helped fix up Natallia and assisted Maksim in dreaming up an alibi on behalf of his son. Natallia had trouble arguing her case because, thanks to Doc's drugs mixed with her alcohol, she had trouble remembering the exact events of that evening.

Valery, of course, never sees the girl again.

Many months after that awful day, Maksim finally softens, and more concerned than angry, he heads toward Valery's bedroom door. A walk that, for some years, he'd expected never to take again.

He listens and hears what he feared. But this time, he also catches Valery talking between his sobs for the first time. Quietly but audibly.

"Please come back."

VIERA

Four years after Lyra's death

"I tried talking to the boy one day, to explain why I'd shot them. We hadn't talked all that much. I guessed he thought it was because I was angry. He needed to know that they couldn't continue living after what happened. Sol and Luna were as good as dead anyway. But if you knew them well enough, you'd know they'd all crossed a line. In that one fight, they'd turned into killers. No longer simply guard dogs. They'd become a danger to us all. But he got angry, as usual. Shouted. Out of control. *"You didn't need to kill her! It was only a flesh wound,"* he yelled. Then he screamed at me. *"You killed her! Just like you killed Mom!"* I ... got angry at that and smacked him. He hit me back. Once. First time ever.

"I was surprised. Stunned even. But it didn't matter what I felt then. I couldn't let him win that fight. Or any fight. So, I hit him back even harder: Tricked him, tripped him, then hit him. He fell back onto the floor. I pounced on him and kept punching until he raised his hands in defeat. He started crying; that ... broke my heart and I, well, I stood up and helped him up. At that moment, I realized I should have found a better way to raise him. I've always just done what my father taught me. I ..."

There was a long pause before he continued. "Maybe it's the age setting in, making me soft."

"How is he towards you now?"

"It's one step forward, two steps back, Doc. The dog was a brilliant idea. And it worked. Who would ever have guessed it would turn out like this, though? He distanced himself again when Lyra died," Maksim says. "He studies, works, trains ... but hardly speaks with anyone. He visits the clubs occasionally but doesn't go out with girls. It took a whole year before he started joining me at the dinner table again."

"Have you tried taking him out with you? Meetings? Dinner parties?"

"He's too young. Not ready. And in his current state, he'd make a fool of both of us."

"No, he's not too young. He's an adult. And he's your son. People will see it positively—that you have him with you at your side. And he will never find that special someone if he doesn't break out of his routine."

Maksim humphs. "Someone that grabs him," he says, remembering Lyra.

"Exactly. Maybe you could try attending something new to start with. A big event, with many people, so not all the attention is on you two. But nothing so important to your business that it would matter if something went wrong."

Maksim looks at Doc for some time. "Sounds like you could be on to something. Ah, Doc," he says, sighing lightly, smiling a little sadly. "I'm sorry. I've left it too long. And now it seems like I only call you when I need advice or help."

"Well, it is that way. But we're both busy, Maksim, so it's perfectly fine."

"Talking of busy, your last email about the experiments was short. As if you were unhappy about the progress."

"Yes. But that was some time ago, and things have since turned around somewhat. So, I'm more hopeful right now. Coming back to Valery, though, you will need to have a reason why you suddenly start inviting him with you."

"Yes," Maksim says, thinking. "Expansion?"

"Your weapons business has drawn some media attention recent ..."

"It's one hundred percent legitimate! I don't understand all the fuss."

"Nevertheless, don't underestimate it," Doc says, turning his head down and sideways, eyebrows raised as he looks up at Maksim, almost as if giving a warning.

Maksim immediately retaliates with his own stern glance.

Doc's face flushes, and he looks down before continuing. "A children's charity affair is coming up in a few months. A gathering of all the big organizations. My father uses charities as a passive approach to distracting attention from his affairs. A soft cover-up, he calls it. Big donations, promoting goodwill."

"Goodwill," Maksim says, testing the word on his tongue as if acquiring the taste for anchovies.

"And it definitely won't hurt you if something goes wrong there," Doc says. "But goodwill isn't enough. You'll need a reason for taking him."

"True."

"Certainly *not* expansion."

"These charity organizations can get in and out of countries where others cannot," Doc explains.

"Smuggling?"

Doc nods and smiles.

"I couldn't trust him with something like that!"

"And there you have it. It's time to trust the boy and show him you trust him. That's your reason. So, give him an important job to do."

Maksim raises his eyebrows so high you'd think he'd seen his wife's ghost walking through the wall.

So, weeks later, after much conniving and numerous evenings with Doc at dinner, where they openly plan the tactics of smuggling drug ingredients in their various processing phases for Doc to experiment with further, they slowly snag Valery's interest.

"I did a little research," Valery says one day after dinner, sitting with his father and Doc in the drawing room. "I have a list of names of potential targets."

Maksim raises his head and squints down his nose as if scrutinizing a valuable gem through a magnifying glass. "Show me."

Valery digs two folded A-4 pages from his back pocket and hands them to his father.

Maksim studies the pages briefly, then rests them in his lap. "I've been waiting for this," he says.

"For what?"

Maksim frowns and looks at the floor between his knees, hesitating before looking into Valery's eyes. "I've been hard on you over the years," he says. "Maybe too hard. But for good reason. For your good. And I think it paid off. I think you're ready."

"What for?"

"Ready to help me with our business affairs. You've been ready for some time. I've just been waiting for you to show an interest."

Almost unable to control his feelings, Valery looks down. Then he looks up at Doc, who throws him a smile and nods his head. Valery smiles back, his eyes glistening.

"Don't think this is going to be easy," Maksim warns. "And don't think I'm going to go soft on you. This is a high-risk operation we're getting into. You'll need to take it seriously."

Valery nods, a grave expression stripping the joy off his face. "I know, Father."

During the following month, with Doc's help and knowledge of charity associations' affairs, they study every aspect of the fund-raising event and thoroughly check out all the VIPs on Valery's list. Using a team of Maksim's tech-savvy employees, Valery directs the hacking of the event organizer's systems, and then they investigate all the attendees.

Working all hours, almost as if their lives depended on it, they meticulously prepare, planning who they will talk to, who they'll blackmail, and which weaklings they can simply force outright to break the law for them. Not only do they prepare every detail of their visit to the event, but they also plan their strategy for the months to follow.

During the first few days of planning, Doc had already advised Valery, "You'll need to practice your social graces." So, throughout the weeks of preparation, they held dinner parties at home to force a change of scene and practice their small talk. Despite being able to charm the fur from an otter, Valery struggled through those evenings because he hates small talk, but they were necessary if they hoped to succeed. Doc even arranged for dinner one evening as a kind of dress rehearsal with the owner of a small charity mediator organization.

"Wine, ma'am?" the butler asks once they've settled at the table.

"I'll wait for the red, thank you," Viera says, covering her glass. She looks at Maksim. "I have the car, so I shouldn't really drink at all."

"Of course," Maksim says while nodding. "But one won't hurt. Bring the red," he commands and motions to the butler to fetch some.

"Isn't being a charity mediator rather an unusual occupation?" Maksim asks as they wait.

"We're one of a kind, that's for sure. And I doubt we'll ever have any competition. It's a horrible job, and I almost can't imagine how my father got the idea in his head," Viera replies.

"*Almost* can't imagine?" Valery says.

"I have my suspicions."

"Oh?"

"Well, it's, um, a little conspiracy theory-like," she says, her cheeks reddening a little.

"I do love a good conspiracy," Valery says. "Please, tell." He doesn't smile. His eyes don't lose track of hers. On the contrary, he leans forward, raises his eyebrows, and waits until she speaks.

Viera has little choice but to follow through. "A few large organizations suggested it to him. Their public intention was to promote trust and goodwill. I believe it was to cover their tracks. But as he got closer to them, I think he uncovered some secrets they hadn't expected. I believe they arranged for his car accident."

"Oh dear," Valery says. "I'm sorry. I read about that, preparing to choose which charities to consider. But I'd never guessed anything like that."

"Nobody did. They covered it up well."

"That's horrible."

"It is indeed," Maksim says. "I'm surprised you even continued the business."

"I had to wait two years until I came of age. But it was the best way to get to the truth, or so I thought. And my father built up the firm to thirty-five people. They really believe in what they do. I couldn't find it in my heart to cash in and let them go."

"Of course, you couldn't," Valery says. "And did you? Get closer to the truth, I mean."

Viera shakes her head, her lips turned down. "I don't have contacts like my father did. And the few employees he entrusted with his information didn't trust me, which was no surprise. It's a risky business.

"And I'm not as clever as he was. The little I've achieved has been an uphill struggle."

"I'm sure you're plenty clever enough, my dear. Why did you think we invited you?" Maksim says, beaming his wide, charming smile. "You may be beautiful and enchanting, but it's your knowledge and your brain we're interested in."

Viera's face turns bright red. "Hah! Well, I'm sure it's not my looks. So, what do you need my brain for?"

"We have a list of organizations that Maksim is considering for a donation," Doc says. They'd earlier agreed that he'd take this part of the conversation.

"We'd like your advice on which ones ... let's say, will use the funds wisely. If that makes sense?"

"Oh, it certainly does. Do you have the list?"

The dinner was a great success. They got information from Viera that confirmed their suspicions and helped them refine their event plans. And it was a pleasant affair. The lively discussion had gotten Valery's blood rushing such that he ordered a driver to take him to the club after half an hour of pacing the carpet. Two girls weren't enough for him that night, so he sent for a third.

On the day of the charity event, Valery greeted Viera warmly. It was almost like meeting an old friend, although he did also follow Doc's warning. "If you see her, don't spend too much time with her. She's a bit of a pariah in the business. It's best not to be seen too close to her. That might bring unwanted attention," Doc had said.

"Shall I show you around?" Viera says, snagging a juice cocktail from a passing tray.

Valery cranes his neck to watch Maksim's progress through the crowd. "I think I should stay with my father. I'm afraid he has rather high and rigid expectations of me." He shrugs, noticing Viera looks a little discouraged, staring at the floor with pursed lips turning down. "And we expect to have a busy day here. What about if you and I catch up for dinner sometime?"

Viera immediately perks up, nods, and smiles, the glint in her eyes reflecting in his. "I'd like that. You know where to find me."

"I do, and I'll be in touch. And maybe I'll see you around later." Then, throwing caution to the wind, he places his hands on her shoulders and pecks her on the cheek before turning away to look for his father.

Two weeks pass before Valery calls Viera.

"How about Grand Cafe?" he says after Viera accepts his dinner suggestion that evening. "I know it's not the current number one. But it has something for almost everyone."

"Oh dear. Driving around that area always confu ..."

"I never drive out to a restaurant. Zero tolerance leaves zero options in my book. And I refuse to have dinner without wine. I'll come and pick you up," Valery says.

"Er ..."

"That's settled then," he says, and she hears the smile on his lips. "Shall we say seven?"

Even before taking their place at the table, Valery orders a whisky aperitif and a vodka martini for Viera. He'd asked her in the limo what her favorite was, explaining how he hated waiting for that first round to arrive. They sit in silence at first, looking around the crowded room, interrupted momentarily by the waiter delivering their drinks. They say cheers, smile at each other warmly, then their eyes begin wandering again as they resume their study of the restaurant's patrons, young and old alike.

"You like people watching, too," Valery says.

Viera nods. "They make me wonder how different my life might have been." Her eyes continue to wander until they settle on Boris just inside the entrance to the dining area. She knows the second guard is protecting the door from the street.

"Do they go with you everywhere?" she says.

Valery follows Viera's gaze. "Yes. He's new, that one. Six months on the job. Still in training."

"He's huge. Isn't he young?"

Shrugging, Valery says, "Eighteen. But *not* to be underestimated. He looks at life through some kind of special glasses. Takes everything deadly seriously. I like him. He's got potential."

An older man and woman draw Viera's attention. She studies them, purses her lips and screws up her chin in her unique peculiar expression while thinking. She humphs. "Sweet old couple," she says quietly, almost absent-mindedly.

Valery tilts his head to one side. "Please don't take this the wrong way, but now I look more closely, I have to agree with my father. You are quite beautiful."

"Hah! You had to look closely, huh," she says, smiling.

"I know it sounds strange, but I feel like I've known you forever. And it's almost as if I've taken your beauty for granted."

"I think I understand. I mean, I feel very comfortable with you, too." She reaches her hand out and rests it over his. "And the last person to call me beautiful was my mother. I was so young I even thought it was true, then."

Valery first smiles, humphs, and shakes his head, but turning somber, he says, "She died young, didn't she?"

Viera nods, eyes and lips down.

"May I ask how?"

"It's ... complicated."

"It's fine," he says, placing his hand lightly over hers. "I shouldn't have asked."

"No, no, it's OK."

"No, it's not," he says, withdrawing his hand, and she follows suit. "How about this?" He breathes in deep and sits upright. "During this, our first dinner, maybe we should agree to stick to happy subjects."

"Second dinner."

"OK, first dinner alone."

"Isn't that called a date?"

"If you don't mind, I'd rather ... well, I'm not ready for ... that, I think."

"Oh?"

"Well ... after ...." Deep breath and a sigh. "The day my dog died, my girlfriend and I fell out, and I haven't seen her since. I ... wasn't really planning on dating yet."

"Oh, I'm sorry to hear that," she says, reaching out her hand again. She wraps it lightly around his closed fist and simply holds on. No accompanying words. No implications. Only warmth. "And of course, I don't mind."

Valery humphs and shakes his head. "Come to think of it, avoiding unhappy subjects will be impossible."

That not-dinner date melts into a succession of evenings so comfort-bound it's as if they wrap up together in warm blankets on the sofa with drinks and snacks and watch their favorite gruesome horror stories unfolding episode by episode and season by never-ending season on a big screen.

The first time Viera came to the house for a not-dinner date, she again didn't want to drink because she'd driven her car. Maksim said that was nonsense and that they have plenty of spare rooms. Valery agreed and had the house staff prepare a bed for her. From then on, those bed chambers became Viera's sleeping quarters and were ready for her every time she visited.

Whether dinner was out or in, once it was over, Viera and Valery would find their way to Valery's private lounge and talk and drink and talk and drink. Viera stops hiding and reveals her liquid soulmate, her solace, her special place as she climbs into and crumples in the bottom of bottle after bottle. Valery also gives in to the white spirit's power while trying to keep up with Viera and admits he is maybe still a little overly dependent on his dead mother, and it still feels as though it were only yesterday.

Viera speaks of her mother's suicide, her strict father and his death, and her dog dying. Valery tells about his training, the story of Lyra's death, his father's beatings, and how his mother comforted him.

He doesn't mention the sock. And she never touches upon her moments in the bath with the pills and alcohol and all the blood. Invariably, one or both of them cry.

At the end of each evening, once Viera couldn't separate one word from another, Valery would help her to her room, ensuring that she never hurt herself along the way. He always left her just inside the door, until the house staff informed him that she didn't always make it to the bed. After that, being sure to leave the door open, he'd lay her fully clothed on the bed, turn on a soft night light, and then go to his own bedroom.

Sometimes, Valery would change and then go directly to a club. His father had many, a few were close by, in town. Other times, Valery would wait until the next day. But he always went.

Almost in passing, one day, at the end of a training session, his father said, "It's OK to use the girls, Valery, but don't put them out of action. They need to earn their keep."

Three years after that first not-dinner date

"It's such a pleasure to see you again, my dear. Three months seems like such a long time ago," Doc says.

"Yes, it does," Viera says. "And our first meeting was so brief. And so sad."

If only you knew. "Yes, well, people's lives these days are so busy that the chance of meeting is like winning a lottery. We should meet like this more often."

"All right, Doc," Maksim says, and smiles, and looks at Viera. "He thinks I should invite him more frequently. You'd think this was the only place he could get a decent meal. Maybe that's why he's so skinny. Only eats dinner once every three months."

Viera snickers.

"Six months, Maksim. Every six months," Doc says.

Maksim rolls his eyes and barks a short laugh. For the past many decades, he'd made a point of inviting Doc and his father every six months. But this time, it's only Doc.

Turning serious, Maksim says, "I'm sorry about your father's business, Doc. Bit of shock that, I imagine."

Doc nods. "I had always expected much more. Well, I've no clue what I will do now. They can't take my private practice; it's my business—not his. But it doesn't earn much."

Doc's few private patients don't consult with him often. He only continues with the practice to keep one toe in the medical world and for access to prescription drugs.

Viera frowns, and her gaze switches between Maksim, Doc, and Valery.

Doc sees her confusion. "After my father died, my dear, I discovered his pharmaceutical business was broke and in debt. Half the people you saw at the funeral were investigating me. Fortunately, they can't come after me for the money. But the business will have to close, I'm afraid. Not that I care too much about that.

"But ..." Doc pauses, then looks at Maksim. "I don't know how I can continue my experiments."

"Experiments?" Viera says.

Valery looks at Maksim; his expression leaves a question hanging in the air. Maksim shrugs and gives an almost imperceptible nod.

"That candy we use sometimes, where do you think that comes from?" Valery says and jerks his head in Doc's direction.

Viera's eyes open wide.

"I've been thinking about that," Maksim says. "Why don't you come over tomorrow so we can discuss it? But let's not talk shop now. Can you keep your horses?"

"I didn't know you have horses!" Viera says. "If I *had* known, I'd have brought dinner to your doorstep every week."

They all laugh, and Doc says, "You're always welcome to ride them while I still have them. They need the exercise."

Later that evening, in Valery's lounge, Viera knocks back a large vodka and eagerly dives back into the subject of Doc's experiments.

"Why didn't you tell me Doc was a pusher?"

"Actually, he isn't. But why would that matter to you? It's not like you have anything to do with him."

"But it's his coke we're snorting!"

"It isn't his. What we use is still from his father's stock. But *he* wasn't big in the business. It was more of a sideline activity. Earning a bit of extra cash, so to speak. Processing a few batches every now and then. Not that it did him any good, so it seems."

"I thought his father was a chemist, wasn't he?" Viera says.

"Exactly. Like everything else, there are good and bad chemists. Doc's father was both."

Viera shakes her head, clearly confused. While she's bought her share of pills and powder, she's never come close to how the drug industry operates. She downs another glass of vodka.

"OK. So, the drugs come from his dead father. Then what are his experiments for?"

"Well, that's classified."

"Oh, come on! You've known me long enough to know you can trust me."

"Trust is not the point, Viera. It's classified. That means it's top secret. Which means no telling anyone."

"I can't believe you won't tell me. Don't you trust me? We've told each other everything up 'til now!"

They both know *that*'s not true.

"Well, it's definitely drug-related. But that's all I can say."

Viera humphs and plops herself down on the sofa, brooding. Silent. Her mind refuses to let it go.

...

"He's making a new one. A new drug! Isn't he?"

"Won't you drop it?"

...

"But for that, he would need raw ingredients, wouldn't he?" Viera says quietly, deep in thought.

Valery rolls his eyes and chuckles. "Stubborn woman." He puts a bottle on the table close to her, and she picks it up, opens it, and pours, unthinking, like an automatic dispensing machine.

"And where would he get those?" She takes her telephone and starts searching the net.

"Are you going to do that all evening?" Valery asks.

Viera puts her phone on the table and stands—a little unsteadily, but she recovers fast. "That charity event three years ago. What was that for?"

"What do you mean?"

"Why were you there?" Talking loudly now. "You and your father don't give a shit about children. Neither does Doc."

"And neither do you! You make your living off their needs."

"You used me, didn't you? To get to people who could get Doc his ingredients. Did you even make a donation?" Yelling now.

"Calm down. You're going to blow a gasket," Valery says.

Viera paces the floor close to Valery. "It's one thing that you lied to me, but you haven't come clean in all these years!"

"We told you ..."

"Oh, shut up! You lied!" She stops right in front of him and looks him in the eye. "And I don't like being lied to!" she almost yells, slapping him hard across his face.

But Valery doesn't flinch or budge an inch. "Viera, stop that. You'll hurt someone if you're n ..."

"Liar!" she yells again and slaps him again even harder.

Valery grabs Viera's right arm, wrapping his strong fingers around her bicep close to the armpit, and stretches out his arm, pushing her backward as he takes one step forward. He slaps her first with an open palm, then backslaps with his knuckles, and her head jerks first one way, then the other. Valery pushes her backward again, sticking out his foot to trip her up.

Falling over her own feet, Viera crashes awkwardly on her side on the soft carpet and lies there, hair covering her face that's pressing against the floor. At least her palms are spread out and helped to break her fall.

"Oh, Viera, I'm sorry," Valery says. "I never meant to ..." He goes down on one knee beside her, strokes the hair from her face, and gently strokes her cheek. "Are you OK? Can you sit up?"

She sits up quickly, considering her situation, and resting on one thigh, she curls up her legs close to her, then reaches out and wraps her arms around Valery's chest. "I'm so sorry," she says, squeezing him tightly. "I don't know why I got so angry." She digs her fingers into his back.

Valery winces but pulls her closer, lifting her slightly and taking her weight with one arm, then, reaching his head back, he looks at Viera's face. "You're bleeding." Gently, he kisses the corner of her lips, licking the blood away, lingering longer than strictly needed, probing a little deeper than maybe he ought.

Viera opens her lips, sucks his tongue into her mouth, goes up on one knee, and flings her other leg around his hip. Even before she's finished, Valery slides his hands up her bare legs, grabs high up under her thighs, fingers rubbing between her legs, and lifts her as she moves until she's pressing herself against him. And she does—press herself against him, again and again, while also struggling to open his pants.

Valery helps her, then twists and practically throws her back onto the floor, and landing above her, he rips off her thong, then she sucks in a huge gasp and digs her fingernails into his back. He cries out in pain. She pulls him deeper. He pushes so hard that she gasps again, then reaches for his hand, wrapping it around her throat and clasping her fingers over his.

Valery learns fast, and with a vicious look on his face, over and over, he squeezes and pushes, and she pulls on his buttocks, Valery squeezing and pushing until Viera struggles for breath. Then she throws her head back, moaning and lifting her hips up to him, and he can control himself no longer.

Two years later

"Ow!"

"Sorry, my dear," Doc says. "You know, one of you will kill the other one day."

"Oh, I don't think so," Viera replies. "We have it under control, mostly."

"Do you? You're coming to me every few weeks now instead of every few months. And your injuries are getting worse. I suppose he doesn't know that you're here?"

Viera shakes her head.

"If you don't tell him, he won't know to be more careful."

That's the whole point, you idiot. "It's fine. I always tell him if it gets too much, and he slows down."

Doc shakes his head in disbelief but keeps quiet. It isn't easy to convince consenting adults. And the fact that he helps her doesn't give him the right to dictate.

"Do you have any more candy for me?"

"You're using more and more, Viera. Is it not becoming a problem?"

"Nah. But helps after a beating. And Valery usually takes more than half of what's left. He's a big guy. Takes a lot to make him high."

Doc opens a drawer in his desk, takes out a key, and walks across the room to his lab door. Viera notices every move he makes.

That evening, having worked himself into an unusual yet righteous fury, under the pretense of bringing a package of drugs, Doc goes to see Valery.

"Here. That's all I've got," he says, handing over two hundred grams. "If you need more, you must go through your father." His words are short and crisp, his tone outright abrupt.

"What's bothering you, Doc?" Valery says, his expression harsh. Anyone not already angry themselves might notice his raised hackles.

"Viera came to see me today."

"Oh?" His eyebrows meet in the middle of his frown.

"Yes. And she was in a hell of a state. Bruises all over her hips and backside. Her neck. Bleeding between her ..."

"Why did she come to you? Doesn't she have a ..."

"She's been coming to me for three years, damn it! Just like your father brought you to me—to fix you up after training.

"What the hell were you thinking, Valery? That she would go to a regular doctor in that state? May as well go to the cops! Are you insane? And what the hell are you doing anyway? You're much bigger than her, with ten times her strength. Are you trying to kill her?" Doc almost shouts.

An ugly scowl races across Valery's face as he takes two rapid steps toward Doc, wraps his right hand around his throat, and lifts and pushes him backward. Doc doesn't need to imagine how Viera must have felt as he tiptoes back until Valery slams him into the wall. He grunts as the impact forces the air from his lungs.

"Watch your tongue, Doc," Valery says, his tone cold and hard and murderous. "Or I'll show you how many times stronger I am than you." And he squeezes his hand around Doc's throat.

Valery's not sure what makes him look; does he hear a hissing sound? Smell something? Hear a dripping noise, something tap, tap, tapping on the floor? Whatever it was doesn't matter. He looks down.

"Oh, for fuck's sake, Doc!" he says and immediately drops Doc squarely back on his feet.

The wet patch on the front of Doc's pants and the small puddle on the hardwood floor continue to get larger.

"Get yourself under control, man!" Valery yells.

Doc crumples into a squatting position, and that helps him get his muscles moving again. Looking down and away from Valery, after a few moments, he says, "I need to go."

"No. Stay here," Valery says. I'll get you a change of clothes. "Then we'll talk. Without getting angry."

Crossing the room to his private bar in his private lounge, Valery pours two vodkas. *Need to be careful now,* he thinks, his anger quickly making way for worry. He knocks back his drink, grabs two tea towels from under the bar, gives the second drink to Doc, and then throws the towels at his feet. *At least it wasn't on the rug.*

"I'll be back. Please wait here, Doc," Valery says before leaving. *Shit. Don't want him running out on me. Or worse—going to Father,* he thinks as he hurries to his bedroom.

Doc sits, still squatting, the toes of his shoes swimming in his piss. His mind, blank, feels like it's racing, getting nowhere, searching for words, thoughts, feelings. Nothing. Finding nothing. Just vaguely racing.

He opens his knees and looks at the puddle. *Oh no.* Shame on top of unhappy humiliation. He sniffles, loud sniffs, and gulps air as if trying to end a short yet heavy bout of crying. He hurriedly puts a hand over his mouth to stop the sniffling. More shame.

Uh, need to move. Sitting here won't help. He stands, and moving the towels with his feet, he swabs up his urine. Slipping off his shoes, he looks at his socks. *Dry, thank God.* He goes to the bar to deposit his glass and find a dry towel; then he leaves the room with shoes in one hand, wet towels in the other, and the dry cloth tucked under his armpit.

Oh, I hope he's still here. Running now, Valery grabs a plastic rubbish bag from under the sink in his bathroom. It's not very big. *It'll have to do.* Then, snatching up the clothes from his bed, he dashes from the room and down the corridor.

Opening the door to his private lounge, he breathes a quiet sigh. "The towels?" he says, searching the floor and then looking at Doc.

"I washed them in the bathroom down the corridor. They're hanging in there."

Valery nods and hands him the small pile of clothing. "I'm sorry, Doc. I shouldn't have gotten so angry with you. I know you only meant it for her own good."

Looking at the floor, Doc gives a single nod.

"Go and change. Then we'll talk some more."

When Doc returns, looking unusually short in the overly large training pants hanging bunched around the elastic closing off the legs at the ankles, Valery says, "Were you able to fix her up?"

Fix her up? Bloody hell! "Yes," Doc says, still not looking directly at Valery. "The bruises and cuts will take a week or two to heal. I gave her some special cream that'll help."

"I guess I should have known she was coming to you."

"She's always welcome. She knows that."

"I could probably use some of the cream myself, sometimes," Valery says.

I doubt that. "I'll get you some."

Valery nods. "And thanks for the coke."

"Your father's starting to ask how much I can produce from the raw materials. He's not stupid. You'll need to watch out."

More nods. A pensive look and scrunching up of chin.

"I didn't know you were such a coke lover?"

"What do you mean?"

"I'm giving Viera more each time I see her. She says you use half of it."

"Hmmm, I'm doing the same. Giving her more, I mean. I only use the stuff once every half year or so. Or less."

"Oh. That's not good."

"I'll talk with her when I see her next. We don't see each other every day. That would be … a little too hard."

Doc nods.

After that, it required many visits before Doc could look Valery in the face without feeling ashamed. And the knowledge of his little accident was a secret they shared and would never forget.

The following week, unexpectedly dropping in at Viera's place, Valery finds unused coke lines spread out on her coffee table.

"What the hell is all this?" Valery says.

"I was about to clear it away. Do you want some?"

"No, I do not! What the hell are you doing with all this stuff? Are you using all of it?" Valery charges into the bathroom, looking for her stash.

It's all laid out on the bathroom countertop. A big white plastic box half filled with small plastic packages. She clearly wasn't expecting someone to see all that.

"You see. I'm not using all of it," Viera says, standing behind him and looking around his shoulder.

"You're using it every day, aren't you? That's no good. This stuff is super addictive. It'll ruin you!" he says, yelling at the end, and he picks up the container.

"What are you doing?" Veria shouts.

Shielding the plastic box in front of his chest, Valery opens the toilet lid, empties the drug sachets into the bowl, and then flushes.

"Stop that!" Viera screams at him while hitting his back and trying to reach around him to grab the box. "Stop it! Stop it! STOP IT!" But it's too late. The stuff has disappeared. Valery turns to show her the empty box.

"You bastard!" she screams, pummeling his chest with her fists. Then, she stops. Turns. And runs into the living room and starts sniffing the lines of coke on the table.

Valery lets her sniff two lines before he brushes the rest into the air.

"Argh!" she screams. "All that wasted money."

"Did you pay for it?"

"That's not the point," she yells, closing her fist and punching him square in the jaw.

Valery's head jerks back a little, but he smiles, then reaches back before backhanding her cheek. The force of his blow flings her over to the sofa, and she lands in a sprawl with her backside in the air and her skirt up high, exposing her bare cheeks.

"I'll make you feel better," Valery says, ripping off her thong.

"No! I don't want to!" Viera yells.

"Yes, you do. I can tell you do," Valery says, his lips curled up in a crooked smile.

"No! No!" she screams.

But he doesn't stop until she's done scratching and screaming, and he's done hitting and pumping.

Viera turns off the shower and checks herself up and down in the mirror. *I should go and see Doc,* she thinks, looking at two ugly cuts on her buttocks. *But I doubt he'll give me any more so soon.*

Throwing a nightgown around her shoulders, she goes out to Valery and studies him sitting comfortably on the very same sofa where he'd violated her. *That was his first time,* she thinks. *And now he has the taste for it; it won't be his last.*

"Are you OK?" he says.

She frowns, screws up her chin and nods. *What the fuck do you care?* "It wasn't fair of you to chuck all that stuff," she says. "I know I need to cut down. But you can't leave me high and dry. You have to give me some more."

"I don't have any."

"Shit."

Silence.

"I need to go to Doc."

"I doubt he'll give you any."

"You cut me. Twice. I don't want it to get infected." She shows him.

He nods multiple times.

She could swear she saw a smile in his eyes. But she says nothing.

"I know where he keeps it."

"Keeps what?"

"The key to his lab. To the drugs."

"You can't be serious?" Valery says, pushing his eyebrows up as high as they can reach.

Viera shrugs. "Can you think of anything else?"

So, after some planning and inviting themselves to dinner that evening, Valery takes Viera to Doc. It's a quiet affair. Small talk about the excellent food and horses and the like is the height of the sparse conversation. The unspoken subjects clearly hinder their communication until Viera winces as she stands to leave the table.

"Are you all right, my dear?" Doc says.

Viera gingerly sits back down again and raises a hand to her mouth, hiding her whimpering.

That wasn't in the plan. Valery rushes around to her and strokes her face and hair.

"I'm sorry," Viera says. "I'm a bit sensitive, and I feel terrible. I think my menstruation is beginning. It hurts like hell. And I think I need your help again, Doc." She looks at Valery, eyebrows raised.

"We, er, met unexpectedly today," Valery says, looking apologetically at Doc. "Well, I was wearing my ring. Didn't really have time to think about taking it off," he says sheepishly.

"Let's go to my office, my dear. You can wait in the lounge," Doc says, looking at Valery.

"I'll be fine," Viera says, rubbing Valery's arm, and he nods.

Once Doc has finished patching her up, he hands Viera a few spare butterfly stitches. "Just in case." He hasn't said anything up until then, hasn't asked any questions, and hasn't tried to lecture her. "They're in an awkward place. The bandages could come loose."

Viera nods. "I'm feeling a little nauseous. Do you have anything for that?"

"Not really, I'm afraid. Why don't you lie in here on the sofa for a while? You can join us in the lounge when you're ready."

"Oh, that would be good."

She smiles weakly back at him as he moves to close the door behind him. Then, holding her breath, she counts to thirty. *Half a minute,* she thinks, recalling their plan, then rushes from the sofa to behind Doc's desk. *Top drawer on the left. At the back.*

She opens the drawer. Her fingers shake as she sticks her hand in. *It's there!* She feels it, grabs it, and pulls the key out. Looking at it briefly, she releases a quick, heavy sigh.

The key fits the lab door perfectly, and within moments, she's inside and hurrying over to the filing cabinet where he got the coke the last time. *Second drawer from the top.* She yanks it open. She stops and stares. *Papers?*

A noise from the far side of the lab distracts Viera. She looks for its source. Rows and columns of cages built into a tall rack. Hundreds of white mice. Some of them are awake and appear to be arguing. *Can they do that?* She can't see properly from this distance, but the remaining mice look asleep. She can't see or count how many are dead, lying there with eyes closed, looking like the rest.

She returns her attention to her search and, shuffling the hanging files back and forth, she peers between them. Nothing. In the top drawer, there's a collection of small plastic boxes and bags with sealing zippers. She pulls open the third drawer. Papers.

Looking around the room, she counts two more filing cabinets. She glances at the clock hanging on the wall, screws up her chin, and shakes her head. Frantic, she slams the third drawer closed and pulls open the fourth and last. Her eyes pop open.

There's a large plastic zipper-sealed bag full of white powder. *Take the whole thing?* she thinks and giggles, then remembers the small bags in the top drawer. Turning, she scours the lab table running down one side of the room and runs over to some shallow built-in drawers.

Bingo! On her second attempt, she finds some utensils. *A spoon.* She grabs it and uses it to fill one of the smaller plastic bags from the top drawer. *Don't spill any, girl.*

Back at home, alone again, Viera stares at the stolen bag. *Maybe fifty grams.*
"Don't use it all at once," Valery had said in the car.

Go fuck yourself, she thinks, preparing for her bath. Her favorite moment of any day is soaking in deep, warm water with the candy running through her veins. She lays out the powder on a saucer, the tiny cooking bowl she uses, the fierce gas lighter, and tourniquet. *Don't know about this, do you?* When everything's ready, she steps into the bath.

An ugly sneer appears on her face as she sits. *He stopped caring the day he started fucking you, girl,* she thinks, not for the first time. *And beating you.*

It's time to finish it, she thinks. She wonders if she has the courage. *Got to at least try.*

"Doc?" Valery says. "It's two thirty! What do you want?"

"I think Viera has been in my lab. No, I'm certain. She's taken some drugs," Doc says.

"Stupid bitch. But can't we do this tomorrow?"

"No. It's a bad batch. Deadly. We need to get it from her before she uses it."

"Oh, fuck," Valery says. *Damn it, I'll bet she's already used it.* "I'll come and get you!"

"No. It'll go faster if we meet there. I'll wait outside."

The hours, days, and weeks that precede and follow the funeral blend into a hazy blur. Valery cries himself to sleep every night, cries and jerks away. *You left me!* He would scream in his thoughts, yanking so hard it hurt like hell, but it's not enough, and he realizes it's because only he is suffering, no one else. There's no one he can smack and blame and hurt and make pay or share his pain.

He misses Lyra. *You let him shoot her!* he screams at Natallia in his mind as he yanks and fucks her again and again until her soul is almost dead, and he's sure she won't do that again! *You left me!* He screams at her as he cries himself to sleep at night.

But mostly, he misses his mother. *You killed her! You let them shoot her! You left me! Please come back!* He cries most nights in his dreams.

They always leave me!

During the daytime, Valery tries not to let it show this time. Not like when Lyra died, or when … His father has started to trust him now, and even though he still treats Valery like a kid, Valery doesn't want to lose the ground he's gained.

Nevertheless, he walks a little slower than usual, head down more than up, not looking directly at anyone unless absolutely needed, lest anyone see his nighttime thoughts screwing with the daytime ones. And Valery starts to see something in his father's plan to fill his life with other things or people he can love. *Oh, I've always known that you planned Lyra with Doc. And Viera—to some extent, at least.*

But I can't trust them! They always leave me! Valery screams in his mind, out of control, and he clenches his fists, forcing himself to calm down and come back to the daytime.

Then, at dinner one evening, his father unwittingly introduces the next step in his failed grand fucking master plan.

"I'm going to check up on a few clubs this evening. Problems with some of the girls. Want to come along?"

Great. Following in Father's footsteps.

NINA

One hundred and four years ago—three years after Viera's death

Is this really as good as it gets? Valery wonders as he quickly washes his lower body, the shower head in his hand, knowingly, stupidly vigorously rubbing in case he's caught something nasty. *No expectations, no disappointments, no one leaving—except me?*

My father's curse. Will I really end up like him? Two whores, two dead whores, two kids?

Since that day his father took him for a drink, with regular visits to the clubs, Valery has managed to tread water. But primarily, he's used his training and work to fight off the darkness. The nights, however, are still the worst.

Earlier that morning, he'd met with his documentation specialist. He asked her to concoct an extraordinary power of attorney for Valery to act on behalf of his sick father—to collect Alena from the hospital when the time came. Doc signed as a specialist witness, as a confirming medical doctor.

With his plan for Alena rapidly evolving, Valery also had the woman begin arrangements for Alena's official papers. They would lie locked in Valery's possession until needed. In a year or so, all the computer records will process and become visible automatically; best not to rush it in case of curious, prying eyes.

When the nurse calls to discuss Alena's release, Valery answers his father's telephone. A few days later, Valery, Doc, and a nanny arrive at the hospital, and shortly after, they take Alena away with them.

They install Alena in the pink room prepared by Maksim's dead woman. The nanny was already settled in the room next door before the baby arrived home.

Looking down at his half-sister in her crib, Valery smiles. *Hell, no,* he thinks. *I'll not end up like him. He never had his Alena. And oh my God, is she cute.*

Nevertheless, Valery quickly gets restless, knowing he doesn't have time for babies, even though he's aware he must spend time with the kid every day if she's to be close to him. *Just like with a dog.* So, he calls for the nanny.

"I want you to arrange a schedule," Valery says. "No diapers, no feeding times, no bath times, in fact, only playing time. And time when she can be with me when I'm working on the computer."

The nanny nods. "I'll come up with some suggestions," she says.

Valery's sense of expectation is so enormous it almost overwhelms him. He can't settle, keeps pacing, racing after his churning thoughts. It's not just Alena, but his plan to take control away from his father that makes him anxious. Yet, that's also exciting. *I wouldn't be surprised if the bastard suddenly wakes up and comes and finds me.*

After Alena falls asleep on her first night in her own home, Valery wants to be doubly sure Maksim won't suddenly wake up and surprise him. Using his phone, he looks at the recently installed security cams, but knows he can't trust all that he sees—not without more time. Doc, who has now moved into the mansion, will also monitor his father's condition from the basement while planning the new lab, or up in his temporary bedroom beside Maksim's. But Valery still doesn't trust the sleeping drug, so he goes to check on his father and pinches his arm hard and unexpectedly. *The bastard's still sleeping*, he thinks, smiling to himself, and he rubs his hands together. *Life is finally changing!*

Time for a special celebration, Valery thinks, and he takes the extra-long trip to the club on the far side of town to see Nina. Attractive and funny, he'd met her the year before, and as he becomes more demanding, more aggressive, she's slowly showing her true colors. Nina makes Valery pay double for the rough stuff and doesn't allow any marking of the goods. "It encourages unwanted attention," she told him. But she loves the choking.

Perfect!

Two years later

Nina had agreed to move to a club much closer, and Valery set her up in a nice place. Now they see each other at least twice a week instead of once a month. It must have been two years later, in the club one evening, when Nina brings a new girl with her into the room.

"I've told you before; I don't want ..." Valery says, immediately angry.

Nina steps up close to Valery and lays her fingers across his lips. "Shhh. This one's special," she whispers in his ear. "I've chosen her carefully. Trust me. You'll see." She knows Valery hates outsiders watching, judging.

Not long after they've started, Valery, already annoyed, starts choking the girl. Nina shakes her head; it's way too early. But Valery, staring first at Nina, then the girl, ignores Nina's warning. He can't stop himself. He wants to see her suffering. However, he takes it carefully initially, and she responds well.

The session continues for a while, all three of them becoming more intense, then slowing up, relaxing, more intense, relaxing, until the new girl seems to faint.

"What the hell! She's not breathing." Valery exclaims.

"When did she stop?" Nina asks.

Valery shakes his head. "Not sure."

Nina punches his arm and puts her ear to the girl's chest. "CPR!" she yells.

They work together for a minute and a half, breathing into her, pumping her heart. It appears it's not Nina's first time. It certainly isn't Valery's. Nina listens as the girl's heart starts working again, and she shows signs of breathing. But she doesn't wake up.

"I'm going to call Doc," Valery says.

Now that Doc lives at the mansion, he arrives at the club within ten minutes, his bag in his hand. After hearing Valery's explanation, Doc pulls out a small bottle and places it directly under the girl's nose. She immediately takes a deep breath and opens her eyes.

Looking at each other, Valery and Nina sigh deeply.

"Here, Doc," Valery says, pouring a glass of vodka. "You've earned it."

"I have told you to be more careful, haven't I?"

"Yes, yes," Valery says, handing over the glass.

Doc stays for a short while, checks the girl over, and does a few basic motor tests, touching finger to nose, etc. "You'll be fine, my dear. And *you* must also be more careful. These games are dangerous," he says while packing up to leave.

"Thanks, Doc," Valery says, then looks at the girl. "Take the evening off," he says, handing her a wad of cash.

She doesn't take the money. "I'm fine, I think. Is it OK if I sit out there for a while?"

Valery nods, takes her by the elbow, and guides her to the door leading to the bar and dance floor, pressing the cash into her palm. "Take it. You earned it."

"She almost died," Nina says once they're alone.

Valery nods.

"Wasn't that a real rush?"

"Well, kind of. It might have been better if I knew it was happening," Valery says.

"Then shouldn't we do it for real?"

Valery looks at her, raised eyebrows, a glint in his eye. *As if she's in my mind.*

"What, kill someone?"

"Why not? There are maybe thousands who don't want to go on living. Millions who don't deserve to. Who's going to miss a few of those?" She grins.

It took them almost a year to prepare, with a few trial runs to perfect their initial methods. Many questions needed answering. Where to find victims? How to lure them? Where to meet and have their sessions? Which type of candidate would make the most exciting victim? They considered different possibilities for finishing them off, and where to dispose of them, although the furnace made that one relatively easy. And not getting caught required careful thought.

Before they even started, Valery dubbed it their "ultimate adrenalin game." That brought a wicked grin to Nina's face.

Years later

The game is a great success. They advance to two, and in the past year, sometimes even three victims in an evening. Of course, they can only play a few rounds each year. They must be careful. Despite the lack of evidence and dead bodies, rumors of a serial killer begin to circulate.

Maksim doesn't notice the furnace being used more frequently than usual: It's at the back of the house, and he's usually fast asleep at that hour. And ash is ash. It gives little away to the naked eye, except when it's piled higher and higher. And this he does see on his walks around the garden.

But Maksim reserves all his energy for Alena, so he thinks nothing of the ash piles. Instead, he thinks about how he can keep his daughter safe from his son.

Valery holds true to his future dream for Alena and spends time with her almost every day. But she's still young, and he's rarely one hundred percent present. He says "Ooh" and "Aah" at the right moments; he plays and talks with her, but his mind is often on other things.

The world has generally become less tolerant over the years. More pastimes that were once pleasures are now deemed illegal, threatening to undermine Valery's family business. And his income. But Valery has evolved a scheme that will address this issue.

"Soon," he says to Nina one evening as they prepare for another round of their ultimate adrenalin game. He often talks to her about his dreams. He has no one else he dares tell so much, except maybe Boris, but that wouldn't be quite the same. "I will sign the purchase order for the drills that will dig my underground world."

"I still don't understand why you're so confident that governments won't simply swoop in and close you down," Nina says.

"That would be like cutting off your nose to spite your face," Valery says. "For example, by stopping whoring to prove that you're better than that. But ending up with no income and starving to death."

"That's not nice!" Nina says, slapping his arm.

"It was an example."

Nina humphs. "And how long before they deliver these drills?"

"Well, that's what's bothering me and holding me back from signing. It's six years, apparently. Way too long."

Maybe it's thoughts about the delivery time that distract Valery that evening. Or perhaps he snorted a little too much, or not enough. But when things turn sour, and Nina's sex partner realizes what's happening, Valery isn't paying attention.

Having retrieved an enormous knife from between the sofa cushions beside her, Nina brings it forward toward her partner's throat. Sensing something, the man lying under her and inside her looks up. He sees the knife, and lightning fast, before she can place the blade securely against his neck, he grabs her hand where it meets her wrist. The knife is centimeters from his throat as he pushes her away.

Nina's face screws up in a terrifying mix of panic, and anger, and fear as she rises up on her knees and puts all her weight into her stretched-out knife arm. "Uuuuuurgh!" she grunts, a long stretched-out groan of exertion as she pushes down on the knife. But the man slaps her elbow pit hard at that exact moment, and the joint gives way. Nina's arm collapses in the middle, and her body falls forward so fast she cannot hold back. The hand holding her knife flies toward her, and the blade sinks deep into Nina's chest, a little to the left side.

It all happens so fast; only the unusual ensuing silence makes Valery realize something is wrong. Valery looks up from his sofa, sees the knife sticking out between Nina's breasts and the man looking over at him—at the knife in his hand. The girl under Valery also notices something is wrong and begins tearing at the fingers around her neck.

Furious in an instant, Valery growls and lifts his left hand, releasing his stranglehold. With the knife in his right, he jabs her throat quickly, in and out again. Not deep, but enough to make the cut he wants. She instinctively puts her hand over the gash as she chokes, drowning in her blood. Valery doesn't wait to see it through.

The guy with Nina pushes her off him and onto the floor. He looks up as Valery crosses the room, naked, blade dripping blood in his hand. He glances at the girl Valery left choking, dying, then whirls back to Nina, dropping to his knees and straddling her.

Wild eyes glaring as he wraps his fingers around the knife protruding from Nina, he puts his other hand flat on Nina's chest, ready to push down. Hurriedly, he turns to check where Valery is as he begins to pull on the handle.

So, he clearly sees the point of Valery's blade passing under his line of vision, watches Valery's face as he feels the knife dig into the side of his neck. Raw, vicious fury mixes with the screaming pain of cold, sharp, hard steel.

Valery grabs the man's hair, forces his head back so he can see his eyes, and presses the blade in using his thigh to help slowly increase the pressure. Painstaking. Deliberate. A steady push. *I want you to feel this, you bastard.*

Then, the man's eyes and expression go blank. The point of Valery's knife has forced between the chinks of the man's spinal cord and severed the nerves of his central nervous system.

But Valery screams and refuses to stop. *"Feel this!"* he yells, and as hard as he can, he slams the knife deeper into the man until the hilt hits the neck's flesh. Valery stares as if waiting, hoping to catch some last reaction despite knowing the guy is dead.

Finally, he shoves the man onto the floor, knife still in its place, and stands upright. He steps over to Nina, pushes her onto her back. *No need to check,* he thinks, clenching his jaw tight. *They always leave me.* And he takes out his phone to send a message: Clean up.

Six months later

Valery sits back after signing the electronic document. Hundreds of millions committed in a single gesture. He stares at the screen, numb, going over the contract in his mind. *I've read those pages a thousand times,* he thinks. *Once more won't help now.* Folding his arms as if to force himself not to browse the pages again, he watches as his Japanese supplier signs.

This is the final meeting of many; technically, it's a formality. A ceremony. A celebration of the deal. The vodka and the sake are already served, and Valery takes up his glass.

"Kanpai!" The video meeting on his screen erupts in a cheerful toast.

"Kanpai," Valery says, raising his glass to the computer. He smiles. *Do or die,* he thinks, and drinks.

Valery had committed to his massive project years ago. The tunnel boring machines play a small yet nevertheless essential part. And though it wouldn't technically finish him, backing out now would cost him dearly.

I just need the old fool to croak before they deliver. And that is also, technically, incorrect. While Maksim is aware of the project and has conceptually approved it, Valery now has almost complete control of the business. So, he can pretty much do as he pleases. *I want The Oasis to be* all *mine,* Valery thinks.

"What does can pee mean?" Alena says, coming up beside Valery.

"I'm working, Sweetie. You should go back to your finger painting until I call you," Valery says, kissing Alena on the forehead.

"It's OK," the Japanese CEO says.

It's not the first time they've met.

"When we say it like that, Alena, kanpai means cheers. But really, it means dry the glass, or empty the glass."

"You didn't empty *your* glass," Alena says, looking at Valery.

The CEO laughs. His team laughs.

Valery chuckles. "There's quite a lot in my glass, Angel." Then, looking back at his computer, "I really should go. We'll be in touch soon, I've no doubt," he says.

"Bye-bye," the Japanese team says, waving at the camera, presumably at Alena, but she's running back to her table.

Valery smiles, then ends the meeting.

"I wanted to say kanpai," Alena complains, holding out her juice and frowning.

Valery looks at her and tilts his head. "Don't pout, my angel. Maybe we can call them next week."

"Yes, yes!" she says, easily convinced. Beaming widely, she spreads her arms and slowly twirls around to return her cup to the table.

Valery sighs. *So innocent compared to me at that age. So well protected. Not like ...*

Then, at that moment, like a sign from the heavens, the sun shines through the window and lights up Alena's hair as she turns back toward Valery. He almost gasps. *Damn, she looks like Mother,* he thinks and remembers how he had that same thought the night Alena was born. *And she will be beautiful. And she will be mine.*

"Come and sit over here, Angel," he says and helps her onto his lap.

Alena's dress gets caught as she climbs up, revealing her bare legs and hips on one side. Then, Valery recalls that moment in the car eight years ago, when he saw a vision of the girl as she was growing up, playing croquet on the grass.

And his mind once again wanders off into the future. This time, it's their wedding night that causes his heart to race, and he has no problem imagining how fine *that* will be.

And she will not reject me or leave me. She loves me.

Riding Talk

Ninety-five years ago

"Why haven't you come to see me this week?" Alena says, standing in front of Doc, lips screwed up, arms crossed, and feet astride.

"Don't pout. And out of my way, little girl. These things are *so* heavy. Shoo, shoo," Doc says, smiling.

Sliding the stall door further open with his foot, he grunts as he lugs the shiny brown saddle onto the small Campeiro's back, then looks at Alena. "Phew," he says, wiping his brow with a handkerchief, then twists the cloth as if squeezing the water out with his fists.

Alena giggles.

Slipping his hand into his jacket pocket, Doc takes out a sugar cube, holds it out on his flat palm, and feeds the treat to the animal. Slowly and firmly, he strokes her, from nose to withers, first right hand, then left, and hugs her briefly, eyes closed as he breathes in her sweet yet musty, radiant smell. Then, he turns to Alena.

"Let's focus on the preparations." He steals a furtive glance up at a camera in one corner of the stall, his gaze returning to the girl. "Not concentrating leads to mistakes, which leads to accidents. And we don't want one of those, do we?" He shakes his head.

"No, no, no," Alena says, still smiling, wagging her finger back and forth with each word. "Can you help me with these?" she asks, pulling down the girth straps.

"Of course, my dear. But first, you try, like I've shown you. I'll help if you get stuck."

Alena prepares her horse quickly, with a little assistance. Doc observes, giving confirming nods each time she looks up at him with raised eyebrows. He tightens the straps after she's pulled them as firmly as she can.

Doc has already saddled up his mare, so within a short while, they leave the courtyard, heading for the lush green fields and vast woodland. Dressed in matching white pants, black boots, jackets, and caps, from a distance, one pair of rider and horse seems almost double the size of the other.

"Let's warm them up," Doc says, and Alena spurs her steed into a gentle trot. Passing through the basic gaits, steadily increasing speed, they take in the scents of the open air and the crops. When they finally reach the forest's edge,

Alena glances at her companion, and he nods, so she initiates the gallop as they've practiced so many times before. She looks again at him, her gaze intense, maintaining her half-seat like a pro, face flushed and eyes gleaming. Doc smiles so widely she can see his teeth.

When they spot the first opening in the trees ahead, they slow up their mounts, ready to cool off a while before dismounting.

"I'm sorry I haven't been to see you this week," Doc says as they walk. "Sit up, young lady," he corrects her, but then smiles when she responds. "That's better. Walking doesn't mean you can get lazy and careless. And heels down, feet further forward. I've told you maybe a hundred million times, my girl. And each time, you forget."

"That's not possible!" Alena cries out, laughing.

"Well, a hundred times, for sure. Now, how was your week?"

"So, why *didn't* you come this week?"

"I have been extremely busy."

"Well, you need to come at least three afternoons next week," Alena says.

"Hmmm. So, are you going to tell me how your week went? And how is your father?"

"Papa is fine, but he's really getting old. He can't play with me. He gets tired. We played chess a lot this week, and I read to him when he wasn't sleeping.

"He wants to teach me but says Valery won't allow it. He says Valery wants to control my life."

Doc raises his eyebrows.

"Papa ... says I need to watch out in case Valery tries to do things with me he shouldn't. But he won't say what he means. He just says I'll know if he does, and I should tell Valery, Stop! Do you know, Doc?"

What the heck is Maksim doing, talking to her about such things? Doc pulls gently on his reins, dismounts, and takes a blanket from the back of his saddle. He throws it on the grass and steps over to help Alena secure her reins on her saddle. The horses know this place well and graze freely.

Finally, while stretching out the blanket on the ground, Doc replies. "If your father says that you'll know, my dear, then I'm sure you will."

"That's not very helpful," Alena says. "Anyway, I was ... er ... sitting on Valery's lap yesterday. I was reading to him. And I could, well ... feel him, moving under me."

The bloody pervert!

"Is that ... one of those things?" Alena asks.

"It could well be. Has it happened before?"

Alena blushes and looks down, lowering her head. "I … wasn't … I didn't …."

"It's all right, my dear," Doc says, wrapping his arm around her shoulder and kissing her head. "You've done nothing wrong. Do you want me to talk to Valery?"

"I … I'm not sure," she says, wiping a tear from her cheek.

"But I suggest you *don't* tell your father about this."

"He also called me Angeli. Twice. He seemed to be thinking about something. I didn't say anything."

Oh my God, what do I say now? "The strangest things trigger people's memories," Doc says. "You, for example, often remind me of the daughter I never had. Now how is that poss …"

"Why did you never have her?"

Why the devil did I say that? "That's a long story, my dear. And not one for today. I may not be as old as your father, but I'm a little tired myself," he says, sitting and lying back on the blanket. He doesn't mention that the daughter he never had also strongly reminds him of his sister.

"Well, I'm not tired!" Alena says and goes off to pet her horse.

Closing his eyes, Doc says, "Stay where I can see you, please," repeating a phrase his mother had often used.

Memory triggers. He humphs quietly.

On these riding trips, he often recalls his mother. It was her, after all, who taught him how to ride. And his sister.

His sister was just one year older than him, and they did everything together. She was strong and brave, whereas he was weak and afraid. They were so close that nothing ever came between them. It was she who helped him overcome his fear of horses. Held his hand, so to speak.

Doc can't recall whether some special event or experience made him afraid of everything. His sister always told him he just needed to find his inner strength; other people, like her, are lucky: They trip over it, although that sometimes gets them into trouble. But he shouldn't give up, she told him. "You'll find it one day," she always said.

Then came the day when she was proven wrong. Intruders burst into the house, three of them. "Where's your father, boy?"

"I don't know," Doc had cried.

Two of them pull his mother and his sister away from him, standing them in front him.

"Tell us, or they die!"

"I … I …"

Then, the sound of something dripping, tap, tap, tapping on the floor.

Doc shudders, feels the wet grass's moisture soaking through the blanket. He rolls onto his side and pushes himself up as if forcefully shoving the memories back into the ground where they belong. It's been decades since he last thought of that day. *Must be Alena stirring things up.*

"What *would* you say to Valery if you spoke with him?" Alena says as Doc comes closer, blanket over his arm.

"I'm not really sure. I'd need to think about it. Do you want me to?"

"I don't know."

"That's quite all right. Tell me if you do. I'll always do what I can to help your papa protect you, my dear. And if it happens again, come to me," he says.

But then his memory triggers again. He recalls the time when he approached Valery about Viera and how he'd pissed his pants then ... just like when ...

Later that day, a message shows up on Doc's phone. It's from Valery: I want to talk with you.

Closing his boss's office door, Doc asks him, "What's on your mind, Valery?"

"What happened while you were out riding?"

"What do you mean? Nothing at all."

"Come on. She always has something to say about me. What did you talk about?" Valery doesn't mention the strange sideways looks Alena gave him all afternoon during her creative session.

"Well, nothing much. Only about Maksim wanting to teach her and you not allowing that."

"You're a lousy liar, Doc. Spit it out."

Doc sighs. "She said she could feel you moving under her. The way she tells it, it sounds like you had an erection while she was on your lap."

"Why didn't you tell me this instead of making me drag it out of you?"

"I promised her I would only talk with you if she wanted me to. She didn't."

Valery takes two quick steps up to Doc and stares him in the eye. "Watch where you put your loyalty, Doc," he says, his tone cold and hard and murderous.

Doc grabs his crotch. *Good thing I recently went to the bathroom.*

"And she doesn't get to decide what adults talk about." Valery doesn't wrap his fingers around Doc's throat this time. Instead, he turns away, stops in front of the window, and stares out. "Besides, don't be daft. She *is* still a baby."

"Nine years old is no baby. And if it's obvious to me, then it will be to everyone," Doc says, his tone hesitant, faltering.

"No. It's you who has such a sick mind. Few people think the way you do, thankfully. You can go now, Doc." *And clean yourself up, you pathetic runt.*

Oh, I'm not the only sick one, Doc thinks as he leaves.

Generation's Passing

Ninety-two years ago

"I love you, Papa," Alena whispers, unfolding her delicate fingers from around his frail hand. Looking down and away for a moment, she releases her hand from his, dries it on the bedsheet with two long swipes, then hooks her fingertips under his.

No one knows why Alena calls him Papa. She had just started one day, and he'd smiled affectionately, and she never stopped. Valery's sure it's something from the TV.

But you told me you wouldn't leave me alone, Alena thinks. *And I believed you then.* A tear crawls its way down her cheek. Alena presses her lips tight again, chin quivering as she studies him silently.

"Shhh, my love," Maksim says, shushing some more while raising a frail, shaking thumb to spread the salty drop over her pale skin. "I'm sorry, Alena," he says, speaking slowly, the S dragged out as he pronounces the word. "I said I wouldn't leave you alone, but ..."

Alena raises a finger to his lips. Her turn to silence him. *Apologize for having me, not for leaving me,* she thinks, but not bitterly.

The glance shared between them carries the words of a hundred previous conversations.

I don't want to leave you with him, Maksim thinks, staring into Alena's eyes. *I should never have promised.* He looks away. *I should never have ...* but now the tears trickle from *his* eyes, tiny pools gathering in his face's deep, cracked creases. He can't bear his thoughts. He had done what he could to save her from this fate, but short of killing his own son, his options were next to none. And killing Valery was close to impossible, especially for an old man stripped of strength and power.

"Shhh, Papa. You should relax," Alena says. *Or you'll have another attack. And I'm not ready ...*

But then the sound of the opening door interrupts her thoughts. Maksim closes his eyes.

"How's he doing, Doc?" Valery asks his private physician while entering the room. *And why is he even still alive?* Despite hearing of his father's condition some hours ago, Valery has only now returned from work.

Doc blushes ever so slightly. "Not well, I'm afraid," he says, his voice soft, head tilted down, looking up at Valery, creating an impression of respect.

Or so Valery thought. *For me? For him?* Valery wonders.

"He's semi-conscious, on and off," Doc continues.

Gently, Valery takes Alena up in his arms. At twelve years old, she's a little big to be picked up like this, but she doesn't complain. Instead, she wraps her legs around his waist, hugs him tightly, and buries her face into his lower neck.

"Such seizures aren't good at any age. And the danger obviously increases when they come together. At eighty-eight, feeling the age as he does, I'm surprised he's survived at all," Doc says.

For a moment, Valery watches nurses fussing around the bed. He can't decide whether they're helping or simply putting on a show. Looking at the digitized displays of Maksim's vitals, Valery only recognizes the heart monitor. *Looks weak,* he thinks, but can't tell for sure.

"They were harsh incidents. I fear his night will be short," Doc says.

"Is Papa going to ... die?" Alena says in Valery's ear.

"We don't know yet, my angel." Valery rarely calls her Alena. He likes to exercise as much influence over her as possible, and he didn't choose her name. "But he might," he says.

Valery is lying, and Alena knows it. Alena understands something of what death means: It's why she never knew her mother.

Alena buries her face into Valery's neck again, and he rocks her, trying to comfort her as she sobs quietly. Her tears drip onto his skin. He shivers.

Moving only his eyes, Valery looks at Doc, a nurse, then back at Doc, and flicks his eyes at the door. Reaching out to the nurse closest by, Doc lays fingers on her wrist and lightly jerks his head toward the doorway. The nurse nods and motions to her colleagues, leaving the room with them silently in tow.

Valery strokes the back of Alena's hair. Glowering first at the equipment, then at Doc, he carefully draws his flattened fingers through the air at neck height, slicing slowly. Doc nods at Valery, then steps from machine to machine and turns each one off. Valery studies him carefully until finally, with a hard glint in his eye and a flick of his hand, he also indicates Doc should leave. *Your fucking drug didn't do the trick. So now I'll deal with it.*

Maksim had suffered acute heart failure and a stroke a few hours earlier, Doc strongly suspected, or so he wrote in the journals. The attacks appeared so close together that it was impossible to tell which came first and if one influenced the other. The response team of five nurses and Doc attended to him immediately. Living and working in Maksim's massive old mansion, ten nurses alternate their on-call shifts so they're always available. Whether they were fast enough to save him still remains to be seen.

After the fateful day twelve years ago that marked the death of Maksim's ex-prostitute lover, the mother of his newly born Alena, the day Maksim hit his son for the last time, Valery effectively forced Maksim to withdraw from everyday life. Under Valery's instructions after their fight, Doc kept Maksim asleep, only barely alive for three whole months. "Coma," was how they explained it.

Maksim's once considerable body mass depleted fast as he slept, replaced by a pitiful gangling shamble of bones that served as hangers for his loose, drooping flesh. For the first time in decades, he felt weak. Motivation failed him with the death of his ex-whore as the last reminder of his beloved wife faded away, leaving him more fragile still. Preparing Alena to survive life after his death was a responsibility that pressed so heavily on Maksim that he could hardly face it. All in all, Maksim's once omnipresent overpowering spirit forsook him, depression took him, and he slowly but surely crumbled from within.

Maksim had spent little time with Valery thesé past years—only upon Valery's request and usually for business matters. Typically, Maksim spent his days with his daughter, or alone. Occasionally, he'd played chess with Doc.

Doc had been around for as long as Valery could remember. Valery never uses his real name; they've always called him Doc. He's the son of a friend of Maksim's father—another one with a Gulag administration imprisonment history. Doc had often attended dinner parties with his father, slowly becoming welcomed into Maksim's greater family circle. This was Doc's ticket into Valery's world because, since Maksim's father's death, Maksim maintained the friendship, albeit on a superficial level. Despite the nineteen-year age difference, Doc and the younger Valery grew closer. No one knew Maksim used Doc to treat Valery's training wounds.

Valery learned to appreciate many of Doc's unique talents and, unbeknown to Maksim, began abusing Doc's services during his later teenage years. Even then, Valery secretly thought of Doc as his private physician. Ever in need of companionship and approval, Doc happily satisfied Valery's needs.

Doc applies his brilliant mind largely to studying chemistry and medicine, particularly the effects of certain drugs on the human brain and body. More than a specialty or vocation, the ability to manipulate human behavior using concocted substances fascinated and invigorated him. That matched well with a branch of Maksim's family business. So, after Valery first consigned his father to Doc's care twelve years ago, Valery persuaded him to remain in his employ as his private physician.

Valery had always hoped to expand the family operation, and considering his father's withdrawal from life generally, he exploited his freedom. Valery set out on a campaign to rule the drug world. He built apartments for Doc and his nurses and constructed a hyper-modern laboratory to work in, all in the unused parts of the mansion's west wing. Valery also designed and dug out an enormous basement lab extending well under the mansion's vast grounds to further keep prying eyes from his projects. This first feat of underground engineering would inspire many future ideas.

With unlimited resources at his disposal, Doc set up his teams of scientists and nurses to discover and invent chemical applications ranging from the sinister and ill-disposed to the benevolent and humane. Valery used humanitarian causes as a cover for the perverse and menacing. This conceptually simple yet immensely complex strategy to execute would become one of the keys to Valery's business successes.

Doc never once contemplated going alone. He could never muster the courage to operate in the criminal world independently. And he would certainly not be brave or foolish enough to defy or betray his boss; he knows him too well for that. No, he's content and busy enough working for Valery.

The recent release of The Fruit opened up new avenues for Doc's macabre explorations and kept him and his team working under pressure ever since. Maksim's frail state added ever increasingly to Doc's load.

Maksim refused to take The Fruit. He said he didn't want to spend eternity as a decrepit, incontinent fool, living constantly in fear of the day that someone would overthrow him. Alena was the only one who tried to persuade him otherwise.

Maksim focused on Alena's upbringing and tried as best he could to somehow compensate for the lack of a mother. If possible, he would've also taken on her education, but many obstacles prevented this, and he didn't have the energy to tackle them, Valery being the most obvious hurdle.

Although Valery tried to hide it, to Maksim's mind, Valery's weakness for his mother and his idolizing her memory was unhealthy—an obsession becoming ever more perverse with each passing year. Maksim often wondered if the beatings and the rigorous education he'd dealt Valery as a young boy had caused his mind to twist that way. He became convinced that Valery had transferred his ungodly adoration of his mother onto his half-sister, Alena.

So, Maksim dedicated his remaining life to protecting Alena from Valery, even though, deliberately hidden deep in his heart, he knew he'd lost hope. He'd secretly given up on saving her because, all too late, he'd realized he'd unintentionally born her straight into the arms of a hungry wolf with no means of escape. This was the very reason his spirit had left him.

At the sound of the door latch clicking closed, Maksim opens his eyes and looks at Alena in his son's arms, her brother's arms, and his body stiffens. As if sensing the change in his father, Valery looks directly into his eyes and sneers at him.

Valery slides Alena's skirt up her bare leg with his left hand, his thumb slipping under her panties as he cups her left buttock and gently squeezes. A small slit appears between his thick lips as he licks them and smiles at his father. Then he begins to rub his fingers up and down Alena's back. If she wasn't just twelve years old, one might be mindful of the first strokes of foreplay.

Roused by what anger he can still muster, Maksim clenches his jaw, feels his blood boil, and throws a look that could kill at his son.

I should *have killed you!* he thinks.

But then, something rips fiercely inside him, and Maksim doesn't have the strength or will to react, and his vision rapidly fails him. As Maksim's life departs this world, all he sees is his son's vindictive glare, and he prays: *Oh God, let there be no such thing as an afterlife.*

Valery turns and carries the twelve-year-old girl out of the room. Passing through the doorway, Alena lifts her eyes and looks at her father one last time. Then, sobbing heavily, she commits herself deeper into the hug with her brother, even though Maksim had taught her she shouldn't.

But without you, Papa, she thinks, *I'll be all alone. With Valery, I won't be.*

So, all of Maksim's teachings and warnings only served to prepare Alena for what she feels she now must do to survive. But in her deliberately preserved innocence, she still has not the slightest inkling of what might come.

"I don't want to sleep in my bed tonight," she says through tears as Valery walks her to the sleeping quarters.

"Where do you want to sleep?" he says, stopping to look at her.

"Can I sleep in your bed?"

After a moment, Valery says, "You can, for tonight." Then he hugs her and continues walking.

"But I want to sleep in your bed always," she says. "I don't want to be alone."

"Well, we'll have to talk about that. It would have to be our secret," Valery says.

"I can keep a secret," Alena says, sitting upright in his arms.

"For always?"

"Forever!" she says and leans back to look him in the eye, challenging his right to doubt her.

Valery chuckles and reaches up to stroke her cheek. "OK, OK. Always," he says, smiling, and she gives him an extra big hug as they step into the lair of the hungry wolf.

This might be easier than I'd imagined.

RIDING TALK

Ninety-one years ago

The evening sun flashes through the trees, catching Alena's hair, and Doc blinks. *My God, she looks so like Angeli sometimes.*

Alena finishes securing the reins and turns to look around the clearing. Closing her eyes, she breathes in deeply, a gesture that would usually bring a broad smile to her face. She adores the smell of the forest. Instead, she sighs, her lips turned down, and then looks up at Doc.

"Don't get upset with *me*, girl. I'm only trying to help you," he says.

"Exactly. You always say you'll help me. But you never *do* anything!" Alena blurts out, then starts crying.

"I said I'd help you where I can. But I cannot challenge Valery. He'd kill me if I tried to come between you and him.

"But if he comes complaining to me about you, then it means you really need to be more careful. I've told you not to mention your father when talking to Valery. And never tell him the things Maksim taught you!"

Alena snivels some more, and Doc's eyebrows gather above his nose in a pained frown. He wraps an arm around her shoulder and gently strokes her face with his knuckles.

"I told him that he was being paranoid, and now he's starting to mistrust me. You *must* be more careful," he says, his tone gentler than before.

Alena nods a few times.

"It's safe out here in the forest, Alena. You know we can talk freely here. If you don't talk to me, I cannot help you."

"So? Did something happen?"

"I was in bed. Two nights ago. He ... asked me why I was still sleeping with panties on. Said that I was a big girl and didn't need them."

"And?"

"And then ... he took them off, and ... he touched me."

Oh, no! Doc thinks, and he almost loses control of his bladder. *Someone should shoot the bastard!* But he hides his reactions. *Self-preservation. You can't help her if you're dead.*

"What did you do?" he says.

"I turned away from him, of course."

"And?"

"And what?"

"What else? What happened?"

"Oh. Well, when I turned away, I ... kind of said, Papa said. And he got upset. Got angry. Then I started crying, and he left."

"Oh dear," Doc says. "Oh! I need to pee," he says, grabbing his crotch, and he jumps up and runs over to the nearest tree.

"Has he ever done anything like that before?" he says when he returns.

"In the bath sometimes ..."

They talk for an hour or more until Doc senses that Alena has had enough. But she's still not done weeping. *I fear she'll always be crying,* he thinks, his heart almost breaking.

"Many people don't get to live the life they want to, my dear," he explains. "And most times, I believe there aren't many choices for them. They can either accept it or get away from it. They'll usually be miserable if they don't accept it and stay. But often, getting away has a very high cost."

"How much?"

"It's hard to explain, but it isn't always about money. For some, it can even mean dying."

"Oh, dear," she says, frowning and looking away.

"Don't worry, my dear. I think Valery has a long-term plan for you. I ..."

"Like an arranged marriage?" she says, turning back, looking at him.

"Oh, no! That's something entirely different, my dear. Where on earth did you get that idea?"

"He's talked about getting married one day. He said in some countries people don't have much choice. That everything is arranged for them."

Oh my God! "I think you probably misunderstood, Sweetie. I mean ... well, I'm not sure what I mean. But no matter what it is, I don't think he will let you get away. So, I think you'll have to learn to accept it."

Alena looks so glum that he is certain her heart's breaking, also.

After reporting to Valery, a mostly mono-directional dialogue, Doc tried to bury his thoughts in work. It is well past dinner time, in fact, close to midnight when he gives up. No matter how hard he tries, he cannot focus.

Instead, he installs himself in a luxury basement lounge with a well-stocked bar. The sitting room and adjacent gym are recreational areas for the scientists and nurses who work for Valery—under Doc's management.

He never gives or asks anything, Doc wonders, recalling the conversation with Valery as he takes a vodka bottle and glass to the low coffee table in front of the sofa. *Marriage? Is that why he's holding his cards so close?* Back at the bar, he pulls a beer from the tap, then sets it beside the vodka glass.

One bottle, one empty glass, one beer. He doesn't expect company; the other staff always use the upstairs games room and bar in the evenings.

He sits, pours a large one, sips his beer, takes up his vodka, then slowly leans back into the firm yet welcoming cushions. He rests the vodka glass on the sofa seat beside him, lightly clasped in his fingers. He gazes out at ... nothing.

He stares, his mind blank, still trying to hold off those thoughts. *Why won't they leave me alone?*

He raises his glass, looks into it. *It's Alena.*

He drinks a generous gulp and holds it in his mouth. It prickles on his tongue. *I should do something.*

He swallows. *But what can I do?*

He sets the glass back on the sofa and closes his eyes.

I can't do anything!

The scene before him changes instantly.

"Come, come! Into the kitchen. Hide in the pantry," his mother whispers, pulling Doc and his sister behind her.

But as the door swings closed behind them, a voice calls out. "There they are!"

A shot fires from the other side of the kitchen door. A thudding sound. A loud, terrified screaming. Another shot.

"It'll be OK," his big sister says in his ear and hugs him tight. But her voice doesn't sound as firm and confident as usual.

The left kitchen door smashes open. "We got them," an enormous man shouts out.

The right kitchen door slams open, and two men barge through. The three men gather around the frightened family.

"Where's your father, boy?" one man says.

"I don't know," the boy cries.

The man motions with his head at the boy's mother and sister, then looks and thrusts his chin a bit farther into the kitchen. His companions pull Doc's mother and sister a few meters away, and standing behind them, they display them in front of the boy.

"Tell us, or they die!" the man in charge says.

"I ... I ..."

Then, the sound of something dripping, tap, tap, tapping on the floor.

"You little pig," the man says. "Pissing where you eat." And he wallops the boy's cheek.

Glancing around the kitchen, he thrusts his head at the big guy, then at some knives on a magnet on the wall. Doc's mother has to lean with him as the big guy reaches out and takes two medium-sized knives. He hands one to his partner.

"On your knees," the big guy says, putting all his weight on her shoulders. He puts one foot on her calf behind her bent knee and lays the blade against her throat.

"One more chance. Tell us, or they die!" the man in charge says.

The boy whimpers and shakes his head. "I don't …"

The man thrusts his head once more. This time at Doc's mother. The big guy grins and slaps his palm on the woman's forehead, pulling her head back.

The woman grunts and tries to fight back, but the big guy is massive and has a good hold on her. Without hesitation or a second thought, he slowly slices from left to right, specks of blood appearing on her neck as he cuts; then red drips oozing down her throat.

The boy and his sister cry openly, watching as their mother slowly chokes on her blood and then falls to the floor.

"Think again, boy. Where is he?"

Doc looks at his sister, a wild glare in his eyes.

Be strong, she mouths back at him. He purses his lips.

"I … I think he's at the Italian restaurant," he says.

"You're lying, boy. And you're next, after your sister." The man thrusts his chin at the girl.

"No!" the boy yells.

The guy holding his sister aims the point of his knife at the girl's throat and pushes it in slowly.

"Nooooo!" the boy wails over and over, screaming his lungs out as the man pulls the blade out of his sister's neck. He sucks in a loud breath, preparing to scream again, when the man holding him jerks to one side.

Even before the man in charge falls to the floor, the boy sees a red dot appear on the big man's head just before the bullet slams into his brain. Then, the smaller guy's red dot and hole appear. He's still holding the boy's sister upright, and they fall to the hard tiles together. Doc looks again at his sister, puts his fists to the sides of his face, and resumes his wailing. "Nooooo!"

The boy's father rushes up to his wife and cradles her head in his hands. No signs of life. He turns to his daughter. Nothing. Then he stands and shouts at his son while stepping over to him. *Why didn't you do something?*

"Give him a break, Ilia. He's unarmed and only nine. What did you want him to do?"

But the man's not listening. He takes his son's shoulders in his hands and shakes him so violently that his head flies back and forth. "You should've done something!"

But the boy's not listening either. He's still screaming, "Nooooo!" Over and over until finally, his father stops shaking him. And then he cries out, *I couldn't do anything!*"

PAPA WAS RIGHT

Eighty-nine years ago

Memories of the previous evening trouble Alena's dreams until, like thieves prowling in the dark, they scurry to escape her as she wakes. But opening her eyes, the unfamiliar surroundings bring back her nightmare. Instinctively lying still except for small head movements, she studies the room and remembers. Her world had indeed shattered overnight.

We slept in Valery's office complex. Then, recalling how the evening ended, *Papa would kill him if he were here,* Alena thinks, and shudders at the thought.

Small wall lights sparkle off the mirrors. Everything shines and gleams. The paint on the high light-beige walls and even the heavy dark curtains have a moon-like glow. The stark modern furniture and decorations, even the bed and its luxury linen in pale shades of maroon, all her favorite styles and colors, were unsullied until last night. The ceiling corners seem eerily nonexistent as the intricately crafted digital monitors merge seamlessly with the walls. Staring up, Alena watches dusty gray clouds chase each other through the early morning haze.

I don't remember seeing the sky. Alena tries to recall and make out what's real and what's not. But images of a starry night cannot compete with memories of what actually happened.

Valery had been drinking, celebrating the long-awaited construction kickoff of his new business venture. Over thirty years, he'd dreamed, designed, planned, and even practiced for this day, preparing new company structures and financial vehicles for conducting businesses and executing transactions that no one could trace from A to Z.

Like his father and grandfather before him, Valery principally applies his brilliant mind for his own benefit. He builds, buys, reorganizes, and sells companies; most sell fast, some he keeps for a longer time, and a few for the long haul. His ancestors had focused on illegal means of establishing their power base and lining their pockets. But Valery tirelessly strives to create the perfect blend of illegitimate and legitimate.

His single unrivaled combination success is the drug industry. Valery's contribution to the competition-rich pharmaceutical sector continuously makes its mark: the lucrative cover-up. And thanks to some of Doc's other unique products, Valery has taken over a large percentage of the recreational drug distribution within Europe in the past fifteen years alone.

Valery's inheritance, profits, and other assets make him one of the world's wealthiest men. Yet the greatest key to his success and survival he learned from his father: To remain anonymous, stay away from public scrutiny, steer clear of competitors' prying eyes, and most of all, the authorities, at least the honest ones. Valery believes that promoting one's personal success leaves one dangerously exposed.

Of course, in one of his identities, he is somewhat well-known for his charities, his contributions to saving the planet, experiments on emissions and the clean burning of combustion fuels, the successful IT companies he built, and others he ransacked—all mundane, publicly acceptable achievements.

Yet, Valery is not vain concerning his power or wealth; he does not need to see his name on the Fortune Global 500 list (although one of his company's names is there). He remains quietly confident. And ruthless. And invisible, achieving his anonymity by adopting multiple identities. The characters he displays publicly are quite different from the faces he shows most other times.

Among the rare breed of the truly financially independent, Valery never borrows, not even for the mega-million and multi-billion-dollar contracts and projects he commissions. He commands total control in his relationships with financial institutions, which is unusual even among the rich.

And now the next wave begins, Valery thinks, swallowed up by his lusciously soft yet firm office chair, looking out into the gray pre-dawn sky and gently rocking to and fro. *My biggest secret so far,* he thinks, smiling broadly. *But what a nightmare expense. The cost of silence almost exceeds the project itself.*

He chuckles at his little exaggeration as he pictures his specially designed Roboids shooting in their murderous ID chip tracking devices, one by one, into the rows of workers lined up like convicts waiting for their food and hoping it'll be edible. This version of his ID chip is crude and too large but still inserts painlessly through the nose in a fashion similar to neuroendoscopic techniques. Yet the risk of death, albeit small, is still too high.

Can't go killing off the clients.

Subsequently, Valery throws billions into his scientists' projects in search of more reliable routes to the brain using smaller micro and nanotechnology. They only need to be big enough to hold a little data, exchange a few simple signals and commands, and hold enough power to kill.

And can't open for business until that's complete. Everyone who enters must get one! Valery thinks.

He imagines a massive rotating globe sporting millions of tiny blinking lights centered in Europe, with millions more spread across the planet.

Valery sneers a little as he tries to compare the size of his tunnels to our Earth's immense size, but then he gives up. *Insignificant, despite their extra length. Probably a good thing, though,* he thinks, swiveling aimlessly in his chair and letting his mind wander.

Years earlier, when The Fruit was first released, Valery immediately doubled his order of drilling machines and vastly extended the plans for his new tunnels, even though he still doesn't yet benefit from the wonder drug himself. *I have time. And what I can achieve in a few short years is incredible.*

Valery had commissioned the design of the tunnel boring machines, or TBMs, then used his new Japanese business connections and deals to initiate fresh opportunities in numerous new markets and businesses. Shipping was one of them.

Without involving his Japanese drilling manufacturer, Valery arranged long-term haulage deals to transport, among other things, the tunneling machines to Europe. The shiny new contracts with the shipping companies acted as a cover for slipping all manner of illicit products across borders that were usually unbreachable. *I should expand on that concept,* he thinks, as his mind slowly returns to the previous day's events.

Yesterday, seven years after the design started, Valery stood in quiet awe behind the crane-mounted remote-control panel. He increased pressure on the large green button, and two of his four new-wave TBMs fired up. The drill heads started turning as the gigantic machines warmed up in preparation for their long creative journey on the first stage of building Valery's underworld, "The Devil's Oasis," as he secretly calls it.

My god, those things are massive! Valery thinks, recalling them in his mind's eye. Standing eleven meters high on the mobile construction frame, he'd reached out and placed a hand almost gingerly on the very end of the drill before him. *It doesn't even look sharp,* he'd thought.

Valery chuckles at the memory. He knew they didn't have an *actual* point. Yet, intimidated by a sense of the force behind the combined destructive-constructive power of the machines, he'd had to repress a shiver down his spine. Looking over at the second machine, Valery couldn't see the end of the one-hundred-and-twenty-seven-meter-long monster digging worm.

Valery knew he was looking at the largest, fastest, most modern, and most expensive tunnel boring machines ever built. The half-year delay in converting to the new self-sustaining Nu-Li-Aerially-powered energy source was worth the wait. As a result, these monster worms, now lined up to construct two underground systems from Ukraine to Czechia, should complete their task a year ahead of schedule.

All my own design. Conceptually, anyway. Valery smiles.

Nine smaller versions of the TBMs will act as the cover project, digging train tunnels fifty meters under the surface, starting from Ukraine, passing under Slovakia through to Czechia, and breaking out into Hungary and Poland along the way. It was easy to buy off the authorities to approve the dig. Valery had spared them the need to fork out precious government funding, but they'd still gain from the profits. Easy money. And all officials involved earned their share in required payoffs.

During their dig, some of the nine boring machines will dive down at various locations to build hidden connecting tunnels to the secret underworld construction one hundred and seventy-five meters deeper under the surface.

Including a healthy buffer for delays, it should take five years for two larger machines to complete the first stage and reach a central meeting point. Digging in secret, two hundred and twenty-five meters below the surface, they'll build a double-arched, forty-meter-wide, twenty-two-meter high, two-hundred-and-ninety-kilometer-long tunnel. Two more machines will start from the Czechia side, and all four will meet in the middle. Then, reducing their size to maneuver through the new tunnels, the TBMs will break out, turn, and expand again as they dig new tunnels to Hungary and Poland.

After the initial main tunnels are built, the drilling of the occupation areas will commence. Driving back and forth, the TBMs will break out in pairs and dig numerous overlapping massive figure-eight-shaped and circular tunnels on each side of the central passageway. They'll link the newly built tunnels and create a complex network of underground caverns and thoroughfares, all connected with the latest technology railways and flight routes and filled with residential and business complexes.

The planned cost for the drilling and construction redefines unfathomable, and the project will run for twenty years, requiring Valery to exercise more patience than usual. But the first living areas should be ready for occupation at the end of year seven, the offices and industrial areas following a year later.

A considerable chunk of my savings, Valery thinks. *But plenty left and more to make,* he chuckles silently.

Secluded forests protect all the secret drilling sites' entrances a kilometer from the publicly visible digs. An expansive sheet of hi-tech skyward-facing screens hovers above the trees to cover the construction sites and reflects a view of trees similar to those below. Valery built temporary living quarters under these shelters for the employees who signed over their souls as the first migrants to Valery's new world.

The laborers will never return home from these forests, and once underground, they'll never surface again: They signed up for a lifetime commitment. Many had been criminals for a long time, more than a thousand others, mostly paupers and homeless, had signed up for a life-improving career change, and thousands more would follow in the coming years.

But workers are easy to find here. Everyone wants off the breadline, Valery thinks as he shrugs off further thoughts of the expense. However, thinking of money and costs causes Valery's mind to wander to the relatively cheap yet inordinately costly revamping of the guest suite under his office building.

More than a million, just for her favorite colors, he muses, shaking his head. *Although I suppose I did add a few things of my own,* he smiles. *Cost almost as much as my private suite. I hope she appreciates it.* As he imagines looking around the bedroom, his gaze flits around his office until he notices the small, polished, wood-inlaid digital clock on his desk. *Damn, need to prepare before she wakes up.*

Still hung over, Valery recalls the previous evening and Alena crying out. *It was the vodka,* he thinks. *Too much always makes me a little careless. But my-oh-my, it was good. I've waited for that for years.* He rocks in his chair contentedly.

Hmmm, but not long enough, he scolds himself. *Well, I'm not going back now. Just need to make sure I'm home free for the next year,* and he calls his private physician.

"Doc, can you come to the office?" Valery says.

"Sure. I can be there in fifteen minutes. What do you need?"

"Er, things have changed quite unexpectedly between Alena and me," Valery says. "Our relationship has become, er, let's say, more physical. Can you bring a morning-after pill or something to that effect? And something that'll work for the next year? Preferably something she can't forget to use," he asks. "Don't want any underage accidents."

"Thirty minutes, Valery. I'll be there in half an hour," Doc replies.

"Oh, and Doc, I, er, think I may have been a little rough last night," Valery says sheepishly.

"Hmmm, you were drunk when I left," Doc says, almost admonishing him.

"Exactly."

Valery prepares strong coffee and then flicks through some papers while waiting for Doc to make the short trip from the mansion to the office. But he's somehow impatient or agitated. Valery's mind flies from one topic to another;

he stands, paces the room, and sits back down again. He slowly settles on the subject of Alena and their life together. A nagging feeling that's been growing these past few years comes back now to bug him. This time, however, he puts words to it.

It's as if she resents it—our relationship. And Alena's words from the previous night rerun through his mind.

"You said you'd take care of me. But ... these things we do ... and ... that hurt! ... A lot!" she'd said to Valery, crying.

"But I do take care of you, my angel. And I'm sorry; I didn't want to hurt you. But the first time always hurts. It'll pass soon enough," Valery had said gently. "Here, take this." Then he'd given her a painkiller spiced with a strong sedative to make her sleep. Using Doc's drug cocktails is his easy way out.

It's as if she realizes. Like she's always realized. But wasn't she too young, too young to really know anything?

Interrupting Valery's disturbed thoughts, Doc knocks and enters.

"I have everything. She can use this for years, if need be," he says to Valery and shows him a small plastic box that Valery assumes contains some kind of contraceptive. "It's an advanced device that can stay in place longer than most. But I'll need to check on her regularly. Use this before, er, going to bed." Doc hands Valery a small remote device with a single button. The devices and methods he designs for application are as advanced as the drugs themselves. "Is she awake?"

Swiveling the screen on his desk, Valery zooms in on Alena lying motionless on the bed, eyes open and looking at the electronic panels in the ceiling. Two tears, one from the corner of each eye, run down the sides of her face.

Doc pretends not to notice. "Let's go to her," he says.

Valery crosses the bedroom, sits beside Alena, and, taking her hand, gently kisses her forehead.

"I'm sorry, Angel. I drank too much last night," he whispers. "Doc will make sure you're OK," he continues, smiling at her, looking deep into her eyes. But he sees nothing, and his expression hardens a fraction. Alena notices and tries to smile back but fails to satisfy him, she sees.

"It still hurts," she whispers, trying to contain the sobbing that's visibly waiting to burst from her, but Doc hears, and Valery moves away as he steps over to Alena's side.

"I'll need to examine you, my dear," he says warmly.

Doc has always had a soft spot for Alena, and Valery is ever aware of it, so he keeps vigil from a distance as Doc goes about his work.

A while later, Doc stands, crosses over to the door, and motions Valery to join him. Valery's feet fall lightly on the soft carpet as he listens to Alena, her head turned away from him, lightly snoring as he leaves the room.

"I gave her a sedative to insert the device; she'll sleep roughly twenty-four hours. I also gave her a painkiller that'll last two days, but she'll be past the worst when she wakes. And a morning-after pill, so she should be safe from conception. There's a cream on her bedside table. It will help the bruising and also works as a local anesthetic. I'll come by later and check on her," Doc says.

"Thanks, Doc."

"You should be more careful, Valery. She's your half-sister; you should remember that. And for even the leanest of judges, this is rape. Rape of a minor ...."

"I'm fully aware of the law!"

"I know that, Valery!" Doc says.

He never confronts Valery in this manner, but his red cheeks and tone surprise Valery.

You'd think it was his *sister I'd slept with,* Valery thinks, but he does nothing to correct Doc. He knows that somebody even threatening to assault Doc would reduce him to a weeping, pant-pissing glob of shivering slime, unable to produce a single spark of anger. That would help nothing. And Valery needs him more than ever right now.

"But she's underage, a child, goddammit! And even in this god-forsaken country, that's not acceptable. And you could never have a formal relationship with your sister. That's also illegal—even for you!"

"Oh, I arranged it in the year of her birth, Doc. It will be legal," Valery says, spelling it out in a harsh, determined tone. *Expensive documents those,* he thinks. *But worth every penny.* Inwardly, Valery sneers while watching Doc process his words.

Things that had troubled Doc for years become clear: The sleeping in the same room, the private tuition in that prudish girls-only school, the constant female bodyguard, and many more minor details. *He planned the whole thing from the beginning.*

"That's why she mustn't get pregnant before she's sixteen. That would spoil everything," Valery says, smiling as if explaining something to a child about to get a spanking if they don't stop being annoying.

Doc nods. "Still, best be careful," he says, looking down and almost mumbling. "Don't want you getting into trouble."

Finally waking mid-morning of the next day, Alena lies still for as long as she's able, uncertain which way to turn her head to avoid the cameras as tears pour down her face. But Valery sees that she's awake and rushes to her.

"Alena, my angel, are you feeling better?" he says, taking her hand.

"It still hurts," she complains. "Just not so much."

Not even a "nice to see you." Valery bristles immediately. "Have you used the cream Doc gave you?"

"Yes, just now."

"Good. Best you stay indoors and rest until you feel fit again," Valery says, gently stroking her cheek. His hand slides slowly down her neck to her chest and then breast, his fingers tweaking her nipple through her thin nightdress. "No need to rush home. Doc said no horse riding for a few days," Valery says, lying. He doesn't know what else to say.

Alena nods, speechless.

Later that evening, excited by his pumped-up expectations, Valery goes to Alena, undresses, sits to remove his underwear, and climbs into bed beside her.

"You look a lot better!" he says, smiling.

"I'm bored," she says.

"If you want, we could return home tomorrow. There's much more for you to do there. Have you used Doc's cream recently?" he asks.

"It was a while ago," she says, red-faced and turning her eyes away.

"You should use it more regularly," Valery scolds her gently and swipes up the tube from the bedside table. "Here, let me do it for you. I'll be gentle."

"But Papa ..." she blurts accidentally, then stops instantly.

"Papa what?" he demands.

"Er ..."

"What?" he asks again, attempting to convey impatient interest while hiding his irritation as that nagging feeling returns to bug him again.

"But, er, Papa told me once that not all painkilling creams are good for you," she says, looking away.

Valery easily spots the lie but doesn't want his evening spoiled. *I'll get to the bottom of that another day.*

"I'm sure Doc knows what he's doing," Valery smiles, wearing his fake, wide businessman smile.

Valery slings the open tube back on the table, cream still spilling from the nozzle. He begins to apply the ointment liberally as he lifts himself on top of her. Over and over, Alena repeats Docs' whispered words to herself and forces herself to relax. But she cannot hold back the tears. She notices Valery tries to be gentle, even considerate, yet he ignores her gasps of pain, and a long time passes before he finally rolls over onto his back.

Papa was right, Alena thinks, but then stops herself. It made no difference, she knew. She didn't fully understand what Maksim had meant but feared that soon enough, she might. And she was right, for that moment marked the beginning of a harsh awakening to the true meaning behind her father's warnings.

God Help Baby Sviatlana

Eighty-eight years ago

I need to get away from here. Forever. If I could only kill myself. But I can't. And I don't want to die. No. Either get away or accept I'm stuck with him. Choose, girl.

Alena's lungs tug at the air, the sharp breaths so short that she rushes to suck them in. Alena thought she'd made her decision, but then became afraid and realized she didn't have the means to implement her escape.

If I stay here, he'll easily find me. But if I leave the country, I'll be illegal everywhere I go. I can't get papers. And I can't ask Doc for help; he'd never go against Valery. I'll never survive, she thought.

She'd decided to take it day by day, step by step, and take her chance to escape when the time was right. But despair comes to visit regularly, and now the glaring sunshine and lack of breeze hamper Alena's breathing further in her struggle to keep her thoughts at bay as they relentlessly attack her from every angle.

Something happened last night, Alena thinks. *Valery said I looked pale. But I don't remember going to bed. And he doesn't usually stay with me until I wake up. And he never gets on top of me first thing in the morning. And he was too kind and gentle. What's he up to?*

Alena shudders at the memory of that morning. Sitting on the cushioned garden bench, she slides off her slippers and hugs her knees to her chest. She presses closed eyes against her legs, and rocking back and forth, she tries to force away similar memories of countless nights. *Papa always said he'd control my life.* Alena had come to believe he'd meant the sex. But now, she fears there's more. She sobs quietly.

Alena startles as Doc gently squeezes her shoulder. "Alena, my dear. Whatever is the matter?"

Although she'd called him earlier and invited him to tea in the garden, she wasn't expecting him this early, and he'd walked across the soft, lush grass as if on air.

"Oh, Doc. I, er, I just keep going over things. I, er ... Tea?" Turning her head away, Alena stands to pour, drying a tear on her cheek.

"Yes, thank you," Doc says, observing her as he sits on the bench.

He opens his arms, and she sits, then rests her head on his shoulder. His skinny fingers stroke Alena's long, well-cared-for hair, then he brushes her cheeks with his bony knuckles, waiting until her quiet sobbing subsides. Alena doesn't see the solitary tear that trickles a short way down his cheek, and he easily wipes it away unnoticed.

It's been ten months since that first awful night with Valery in the guest suite of his office, and Alena has sat in Doc's comforting arms many times since. Finally, the distraught girl speaks.

"Something happened last night, didn't it?" Alena says.

Doc sighs inwardly. He hates these conversations. *At least it's me she turns to. Safer.*

"Valery said you weren't feeling well. I helped take you up, gave you something to help you sleep." He avoids the details and certainly doesn't mention the diaphragm. Then his tone changes, and he speaks slower, quieter, his words crisper.

"But you're a *big girl* now. It's *legal* to give you *more* medication and much stronger. It made you sleep *much deeper*," he says, emphasizing some words strangely.

Alena's brow creases as she tries to understand. After some moments, they resume drinking their tea and talking about other things, such as horses.

Sitting in her lounge later, Alena chews over Doc's words. *What did he mean, I'm a big girl now? I'm only sixteen.* She recalls her birthday party—only two days ago.

"You're practically a full-fledged adult," Valery had said to her during his birthday speech.

And almost immediately after, something happened, Alena thinks.

Sixteen, adult? But that's at eighteen. Sixteen, almost fully fledged? I'm not even allowed to buy alcohol at sixteen. Can't leave home, can't get married. Legal? More?

Alena grabs her phone and searches the net: "legal age belarus." General results pages appear first, but she spots the sixth one on the list focusing on Belarus. While reading the article, Alena's eyes widen. Her mouth inches open until she stops reading, holds her breath a moment, and then gasps.

Oh my god, no, no, it can't be. She holds her breath, eyes frantically flitting here and there, then springs to her feet and runs off in search of Doc.

After a few months of waiting and careful monitoring, Valery spots the changes he hoped for: The tell-tale signs. So, one morning, with a spring in his step and especially enjoying the early morning sun, Valery goes to Alena while she lies awake in bed.

"Angel, your monthly cycle is off by three weeks. Is everything OK?" he says.

"Everything's fine, Valery. I'm sure it'll straighten itself out soon." *He's watching for it,* Alena thinks, confirming her suspicions, despite Doc's refusal to answer her truthfully about that strange night three or four months ago.

Valery always monitors and records everything he can, so Doc never steps out of line with Alena. Whenever Alena asks him, he sticks to the story Valery has fed him.

"Come in," Valery calls out in response to a knock on the door, and Doc enters. "Alena, my love, I've asked Doc to give you a checkup. You know how concerned I get sometimes," he says and smiles apologetically.

Alena doesn't protest. She also wants to know.

While she waits, as she occasionally does, Alena takes stock of her life despite her young age, counting the years and noting one positive and one negative thing for each year. *1. I survived; 2. I didn't die; ...* She doesn't reach sixteen before Doc informs her she's with child.

"Congratulations, my angel!" Valery says, play-acting a little. "This will be exciting."

But it sounds silly to Alena, coming from him.

"You'll need to take extra good care of yourself," Doc advises her gently. "These things going wrong can be even more painful than when they go well."

"It makes me nervous," Alena says, looking down and away from them. *Because of what I must do now,* she thinks, and she wonders if Doc suspects.

Valery hides his relief when week twelve's ultrasound shows that the child will be a girl, but he waits for the endorsement from week sixteen's scan before confronting Alena. That same evening, after confirming the girl's gender, Valery places a slim file of papers on his bedside table and then turns to Alena.

"Now that you're carrying my child, I think it's time we got married."

"But we can't get married!" she says, promptly sitting up. "I'm your half-sister. And I'm only sixteen. It would be totally illegal," she protests.

"Alena, my love," Valery says, "life is not always as it seems on the surface. Why do you think I've kept you so close all these years, protected you all this time?"

But Alena's unable to listen as she falls headlong into a panic and fights to avoid crashing to rock bottom. *I thought I had more time. I need more time. I have to find a way out of this!* Her thoughts scurry down corridors and pathways, searching for options, but with each turn, a new door slams in her face.

"Alena?" Valery prompts her, and she forces herself to focus on him.

"What do you mean?" she says.

"Your life isn't as you think it is. Your father could never have told you this, but now it's time for the truth," he says.

"I don't know what you're talking about."

"No, of course not. Let me tell you. My father's woman died at birth, and her baby survived—or so he thought. Distraught by her death, he went home, and I stayed with the baby, but she also died—during her second hour.

"As chance would have it, another woman, a single mother, had died that same night—as if motherhood were going out of fashion." Valery humphs and smiles. "But this baby survived. And she was so beautiful. It was neither difficult nor expensive to persuade the doctor to switch the babies around. Wish I could say the same for the paperwork.

"Anyway, after that day, my father withdrew from pretty much everything. He also wasn't interested in paperwork, so he never saw the versions of documents with your real name. So, you see, being my sister won't prevent us from marrying—because you're not my sister. You're an orphan," Valery says. Lying has become second nature to him.

"And now you're pregnant, you can legally marry before you're eighteen," he explains. "In fact, it's already done. Here are the papers." He takes the immensely costly file from the bedside table and shows her the witnessed wedding certificate.

As Alena listens, Valery's words squeeze the very air from her lungs, little by little, with each syllable. Hardly able to breathe, she tries to object.

"It can't be true. It can't be. Papa would've seen ..."

"Papa didn't know, Angel. He didn't see anything. I was protecting him even as I fell in love with you," he says, like a contented wolf without further need of his sheep's clothing.

Alena begins to wail, quietly at first but with slowly increasing intensity. Valery reaches out with both hands and pulls her to him. Alena doesn't resist, and while Valery gently strokes her neck, he slides out a cocktail patch from the back of the file of papers, peels off the cover, and lightly presses the patch over a vein on her neck. The drug kicks in within a minute, and the overwrought girl calms down and sleeps fast. Valery lays her back onto her pillows a short while later and then leaves the room to go and find Boris.

Valery had long ago selected Boris from the ranks of Maksim's security team and had secretly prepared him for the day Valery would take control of the Serpents, as they were called. That day came when Maksim started his big sleep. Valery was certain that the existing Serpent lead was dedicated to Maksim and would not support him. So, he arranged an accident for him and then promptly promoted Boris.

Boris had led the Serpents for fifteen years under Valery when he was injured in the underground accident. It had cost Boris a leg, his manhood, and a year of his life recuperating. Valery's still coughing up millions in fixing him up, but he considers it a small price to pay to keep that loyal heart beating.

Boris owed his life to Valery, and he didn't think twice when witnessing the wedding papers.

"I need someone to watch over the child. Both now and when she arrives. And an extra pair of eyes on Alena," Valery told him.

Boris had accepted immediately, but Valery had made it easy for him. "You can run the Serpents from the house from now on. But have someone else do the rough stuff for a change," he'd said.

There was no talk of Boris's disabilities. The robotic prosthetic leg was so advanced that Boris was as good as new, and they both knew it. As for Boris's manhood, well, what would anyone say?

When Boris arrived on the scene, Alena's gradually diminishing hopes of influencing her life disappeared entirely. So not long after, the sixteen-year-old, legally wed young woman finally gave birth to a beautiful baby girl.

Clearly, Sviatlana is born of Maksim's line, yet Valery doesn't see it. Cannot see it. Refuses to see it. *She's more beautiful than any of us,* he thinks in wonder. *Everything I wished for.*

Valery falls in love with Sviatlana at first sight, but mainly because that's how he meant it to be; that's how he'd planned it. Yet while gazing upon his daughter-niece, a fierce fire swells up from within, turning Valery's thoughts briefly to the past. He relives his father's beatings, his mother's shooting, and the subsequent years of relentless, scathing bitterness, and he recalls how his father turned Alena against him.

At least that bastard can't infect Sviatlana with his vindictive words, Valery thinks, then huffs, and, nodding to himself, he reaches a decision that's long hung over him. *And I'll not give her whining, spoilt mother the chance to ruin her either,* he thinks, his cold, piercing eyes glaring as his lip curls up on one side. Valery pulls out his phone and first calls his documentation specialist, then, after a long moment, lost deep in thought, he dials Doc.

"Doc, I believe there's something wrong with Alena. I'm going on my morning walk. Meet me in the garden, and I'll explain."

Later, once back in his lab, Doc mulls over Valery's words, careful to hide his thoughts and emotions, for he knows Valery records everything. Tapping on his computer's control panel, he pulls up his very own encyclopedia of drugs: All manner of chemicals used for good and bad. He first lazily browses the entries, scanning the classifications and descriptions, some with his own notes, others showing possible combinations, all with names of producers, some with his name beside them.

But really, he already has an idea of what he's looking for, and finally, he reaches out and types one keyword: Untraceable.

Doc stares at the word for some time before pressing the search button. The resulting list displays quickly.

God help Alena, he thinks. *And God help baby Sviatlana.*

MAMA'S HERE, ANGEL

Eighty-six years ago

What a sickly-looking skinny runt, Valery thinks, forcing back a sneer as the doctor walks in.

"Professor Johansson, thank you for interrupting your busy schedule and coming all this way at such short notice," Valery says, reaching out and vigorously shaking the man's limp, sweaty fingers. *Disgusting.*

"Come in. Please, do sit down," Valery continues, and he waves Johansson and Doc over to luxury wide-armed leather chairs awaiting them in front of his desk. *My god, he's tall,* he thinks, which is saying something because Valery himself is just over two meters.

"I'd have come down to the lab to meet you earlier, but Doc persuaded me to let you work first," Valery says. *And I had better things to do.*

"Yes, we've been busy indeed," Johansson responds. "But unfortunately, we've not turned up any new findings. I've taken fresh blood and other samples that I'll take home and run through some more tests, but these tests could take, er, quite a while, I'm afraid."

"How long?" Valery says, inwardly rolling his eyes.

"Well, genetic and genome testing are complex tasks. Even more so without any prior history. Our cytogenetics lab will look for chromosome-based disorders. Another lab specializing in molecular genetics will analyze the ... er ..."

Valery had glanced aggressively at Doc, and Johansson was astute enough to pick up on it, remembering Doc's warning: "No complex medical or technical terms when addressing Valery." Valery prefers to play dumb to avoid discussing risky details with insignificant nonentities boasting big job titles.

"Er, these tests can take weeks and sometimes months, I'm afraid," the visiting doctor concludes. He fidgets in his chair, his gaze alternating between the floor and Valery.

"What's the problem with that?" Valery asks.

"Er ..."

"Valery," Doc takes over. "Dr. Johansson thinks we may not have months, possibly only weeks," Doc explains. *God, I can't wait until all this play-acting is over.*

"Oh, dear," Valery mutters, and he looks away briefly.

"I'm sorry we can't do more," says Professor Johansson. But he's clearly not planning on carrying this burden alone. "Doc and I will, of course, give these tests our highest priority," he concludes while standing to leave.

"Thank you, Professor," Valery responds quietly, sounding gloomy. *Doc, get this irritating man out of my life!*

Valery watches on the security surveillance cams as the car pulls away with the professor safely inside, headed for the airport. *Just like the others,* he thinks. *Full of himself. Second-rate prick.*

Johansson is the second of the final four specialists Doc is consulting. All experts in rare diseases and hired to analyze Alena's deteriorating condition.

Waiting for Doc to return, Valery thinks through all the steps again. He's kicked himself a hundred times for accepting this complex and time-consuming plan, his irritation now increasing with each passing week. As Doc enters his office, Valery advances on him.

"I've had enough of this ridiculous, bloody elaborate scheme," Valery says.

But Doc sounds curiously confident as he sticks to his guns.

"Elaborate, maybe, but after all the attention she's getting, there's no way anyone will suspect anything. Some of the world's so-called finest will have already looked at her. Case done and dusted."

Deflated, Valery can't think of a strong counterargument. "And you're certain they'll not uncover your cocktail?"

Doc nods vigorously. "One hundred percent. Appelby found nothing. These last two losers will stop after a day when they don't smell a gold mine. The only challenge is Wang. She has looked for a month and a half and shows no signs of giving up. I hadn't expected that.

"But if you can't wait six to ten more months, we could drop this whole plan," Doc says. *Hopefully he'll let that one slip,* he thinks—almost in parallel, then rushes on. "Alena could have a miraculous recovery, and you can find a more direct way to deal with her."

"What the hell do you mean, ten months? You promised me six at most," Valery protests.

Or not. Doc has been trying to prolong the whole affair, desperately hoping to save Alena. He has even contemplated praying to the devil for a miracle; he knows God will not help him. "What difference does it make? Six, ten, does it really matter?"

"You know I want this over with before Belarus enters the EU," Valery says, his face taut, eyes almost crossed under his heavily creased brow. "I don't want her name on any paperwork when we move into the West. It'll complicate things horribly."

"Yes, I remember now. But Wang needs to finish her research. To rush her would be suspicious."

Valery stands and paces the room. *It's not like him to forget details,* he thinks. *Ten months more? What's he thinking?* He paces feverishly. *It's not like she's his woman—or daughter.* Then it dawns on him, or at least he guesses at the problem. Doc has never talked about his feelings for Alena, but Valery's always suspected something and decides delay is not helping. He turns and looks out the window.

"Doc, I know you have a soft spot for Alena."

What would you know? But Doc has long been with Valery and recognizes his decisive tone. Instantly, all hope escapes him, and he dies a little more inside.

"But she's not good for Sviatlana," Valery continues. "The way my father turned Alena against me, that's like a disease. And Alena's infected. Bitter. Angry. I think she even hates me now. She'll turn Sviatlana against me, too, and I'll not risk that for a month longer than necessary.

"I'm sorry, Doc. But I've made up my mind. I hope you're still with me on this," Valery says.

Doc's two options require no explanation. "I may not like it, but yes, of course I'm with you," he says. *And for making me do this, I'll hate you for as long as I can still breathe.*

"Good. Three months tops, Doc. Sviatlana won't even be two by then and will remain untainted. I don't care if you have to ruffle a few spotted bowties. Get it done," Valery commands.

The months fly by after Johansson's fleeting visit, or so it seems to Doc. Still pointlessly prolonging it as long as possible, he painstakingly prepares the contents for Alena's final injection.

He's had many patients destined to die in the past—from Valery's line of business. His lab rats, as he likes to think of them. Vermin to experiment on. Doc maintains his very own sizeable casualty list from failed and successful trials. None, of course, publicized in the reputable medical journals alongside his other famous achievements.

But Doc didn't care about those other patients, and the experiments never bothered him. Alena is something completely different, however, and this task is unbearable.

Valery knows the planned time but hasn't turned up. Doc sends a message asking whether Valery's really sure he doesn't want to be present.

Yes. You say goodbye to her for me, came the response.

I'll never forgive you for putting me through this, you bastard, Doc yells at Valery from within the safe walls of his mind, careful not to express his feelings outwardly. Valery will be recording this, and possibly even watching now.

Doc slowly pushes the needle into the plastic tubing. Then he presses on the syringe, minuscule millimeter by minuscule millimeter, mixing his killer cocktail with the IV fluids, dragging it out for God-only-knows what reason.

Later, he'll keep Alena on life-support, allowing the cocktail time to break down and disappear. That will only require a few hours. It was his research into The Fruit that caused him to chance upon the key ingredients for this killer drug, thus turning a marvel designed to prolong life into something that does quite the opposite. And he's still experimenting. But so far, The Fruit's secrets still evade him.

Doc sits quietly. He stares at Alena. *Farewell, sweetheart. My girl. My sweet, sweet girl.*

A tear runs down his cheek. *I wish I could've saved you, taken better care of you.*

Another tear or two. *I wish your eighteenth had been your first, not your last.* More tears. He doesn't move. He doesn't sob.

He doesn't say anything to her. Not because Valery might hear. But he doesn't want to spoil her dreams or instill any level of consciousness. He doesn't want to remind her she has a life, for she'd surely know he was taking it from her. She'd know that those who should love and care for her, don't. That those with the responsibility and power to protect her were, instead, killing her.

He simply sits, thinking, grieving. Every now and then, more tears roll.

Twenty-one hours later, Doc takes one last blood sample and checks for the presence of his cocktail.

Nothing. She's gone.

Dragging his feet, Doc returns to Alena's bedside and turns off all the machines. Reluctantly, he sends another message to Valery: It's done. *One day, I'll kill you for this!*

Boris flicks off the camera surveillance and locks his phone, leaving Doc to mourn in solitude. Resting back in the chair, feet up, his eyes wander the ceiling for a change.

He wasn't close to Alena and hadn't spent time with her or wanted to. *But I don't understand this,* Boris thinks. He twists his head to the side, looking at

Sviatlana.

Finally. He sighs quietly as if afraid any noise might wake her. He doesn't usually sit with her; he's a bodyguard, not a babysitter. But he succumbed this time when she begged him this evening.

She's changed my life, Boris thinks, studying Sviatlana for some time. *But what will happen to her now her mother is dead?*

Five years later

"I wish Mommy was here," Sviatlana says, looking up from the TV.

"I know. But Mama's here, Angel, inside you," Valery says, placing his huge hand on Sviatlana's young heart. Then he gently lifts her off the sofa and kisses her lips.

"Oh, what a long day it's been. But it was *your* day. And seven years old already. What a big girl you are now. You're practically a full-fledged adult." Valery smiles at her.

Sviatlana beams back at him.

"Come," Valery says. "It's time for bed."

Watching on the security monitor, Boris shakes his head. *Bodyguard,* he reminds himself. *Keep out of this.* "It's not your business," he whispers.

RIDING TALK

Seventy-five years ago

Listening to the thump-beat-stomp of the horse's hooves as if enjoying a classic rock symphony, Doc smiles inwardly. The heavy pounding of Boris's muscular Clydesdale mingles with the Campeiro's lighter stamping as it flies Sviatlana through sun-dazzled trees, accompanied by the racing, rhythmic drumming of his multi-colored Appaloosa.

Being frightened even by shadows, he never used to feel truly comfortable out in the forest alone or with only Alena. But since Boris joined him with Sviatlana, with his mini armory strapped around his being, Doc has enjoyed riding without the worry.

As they slow the horses from a gallop, Sviatlana, riding beside Doc, lands awkwardly on her saddle and winces.

"Are you all right, my dear?" he says.

Sviatlana starts weeping but doesn't say anything. Without moving her head, using eyes only, she indicates behind her, toward Boris.

Hmmm, Doc thinks, then looks back at Boris. "Would you mind giving us a moment?"

Boris nods and slows his horse up. *Bodyguard, not doctor or counselor,* he reminds himself.

When the privacy distance seems enough, Doc says, "What's the problem, my dear?"

"I'm ... well ... bleeding ..." Sviatlana says.

"Ah. You weren't expecting that?"

Sviatlana looks at him, puzzled, and shakes her head.

"Hummm. It's about time someone talked to you about how babies are ..."

"Oh, it's not that, silly! We've been doing it for ages now," Sviatlana says and giggles.

Doc's eyebrows shoot up into his forehead.

"How long?"

"I don't know. A long time. Six or twelve months, maybe."

Oh no! Doc turns to stare at the girl.

"Or two years, or three. I don't remember, but ages."

Oh my God! "Are you in pain?"

"Sometimes."

"Shall we go back?"

Sviatlana shakes her head. "I can manage."

"Well, if you would like, I can give you a checkup later and maybe give you something to help if needed."

"That would be good."

"But you should think about what you plan to tell your father about this."

"What do you mean?"

"Well, it wouldn't be good to hide it for very long. I mean that we've talked and that I'm helping you."

"Oh."

"But I don't think you need to tell him everything, my dear."

Sviatlana's face brightens a little, and she says, "What if I say that I told you I hurt myself riding?"

"Well, that could work for now. But we'll need to talk about this some more."

Later that day, a message arrives on Doc's phone: Smoke? Boris doesn't smoke, but he bums one from Doc every now and then. On good weather days, they walk in the garden, away from the security cameras.

"What was that about earlier?" Boris asks once he's lit up.

"Well, I'm not sure I should say. Although, it's quite shocking, actually."

"I need to know if she's in any danger. It's my job to protect her."

"Of course," Doc says, and then explains what happened during the riding trip, plus some of the things Sviatlana told him later.

"That's insane! I'm going to speak with him!" Boris says.

"I can guarantee that you'll be dead before sundown if you do that. Especially with the mood you're in now. And you can't protect her when you're dead."

Boris rubs his chin and nods. *Hmmm, he has a point. I wouldn't be the first ...*

"And don't underestimate her loyalty to Valery."

Sixteen years later

"This horse must be getting old, fast after carrying me all these years," Boris says, leaning forward to pat the beast on the shoulder.

Doc's expression takes on a sly smile that reaches to his eyes. "Don't be so sure."

"What do you mean?"

"He's been on The Fruit for some time now."

"You didn't!" Sviatlana says. "How do you know it works on animals?"

"I've been testing it, of course. And ..."

"How could you do that? Turn such a beautiful animal as a horse into a lab rat!"

Boris's eyes twinkle as he looks at the beautiful, incensed young woman beside him.

Need to watch that. It's becoming too obvious, Doc thinks, the corners of his lips lifting imperceptibly. "My dear, The Fruit has been available for thirty-four years. And that's exactly how long I've been testing it. On rats first, of course."

"Oh."

"And I know it's hard to tell, but not many horses live past thirty. Your mother's Campeiro there is almost forty." *Damn it. Stupid, loose tongue!*

"You ... you've never told me that before," Sviatlana says, her tone dropping as the joy in her expression disappears.

Boris's face can't decide whether it should frown at Doc or cry on Sviatlana's behalf.

"No. And I'm sorry, my dear; I didn't mean to mention it now, either."

"Why not? I'd have been happy knowing it was hers."

"Well, I wasn't certain of that. And I didn't want to cause you more distress than necessary."

"I will never understand why no one could find out why she died."

Doc nods. "It wasn't for want of trying."

Boris and he exchange furtive glances.

"Not everything can be explained," Boris says.

"But it was certainly tragic and very sad," Doc says.

Boris screws up his chin. "It was."

They ride in respectful silence until the fields come into view. Then, not being one to stay down in the dumps for long, Sviatlana perks up as she harkens to the call of the bright blue open sky.

"Last one back's a sissy!" she says and kicks her horse into a gallop.

They race almost neck and neck until they reach the courtyard, Sviatlana slightly ahead. Then, looking at Boris, Doc jerks his head back, and Sviatlana's lead grows as they slow down. Doc looks straight ahead as he addresses the curious man.

"May I advise you to curb your facial expressions, young man."

Having started on The Fruit when he was thirty-six, Boris will retain his youthful looks forever, it seems.

"I don't mind who you fall for, but Valery might."

Boris's eyes pop open, and he turns to look at Doc. The older man's face sports a tiny smile, then he spurs his horse on.

The message arrives a few hours later: Smoke?

After the usual silent greeting with only a nod or two to confirm the act, the handing over of a cigarette, and having achieved the usual few meters from the building, Boris has something that practically leaps from his tongue.

"She has a nasty bruise on her arm. Looked a couple of days old."

Doc nods slowly. "He's getting more violent. ... I told you he would ... eventually."

"Maybe it's because she's fighting back. They were arguing about marriage. I'm guessing, but it seems like she said no. I heard her say she was too young. We should do something."

"Maybe, indeed. But she's not ready for change yet. If we force anything, we'll lose her if she's not willingly part of it."

Boris purses his lips yet nods. "But she's getting hurt."

"Remember, she is part of those games, too. Besides, he won't hurt her seriously. He needs her too much. But rest assured, I will inform you if there's something important."

"Likewise."

Five years later

"Doc, I need some advice," Sviatlana says as they approach the clearing.

"About what, my dear?"

But Sviatlana stares back at him, then thrusts her head gently in Boris's direction.

"Doctor stuff," he says, looking at Boris.

Boris rolls his eyes. "Fine. I will go and sweep up the horse shit."

Sviatlana giggles. Boris can't hold back his smile.

Once Boris has led their horses out on the grass, Sviatlana finally says, "There's this guy, Doc. He works for Dad. His name's Adam."

Doc's eyes open wide.

"He's ... cute. Nice. I like him."

"You've met him?"

"Yes. Dad introduced us. He said Angelina was a pretty name." Sviatlana smiles.

Following in Valery's family pattern of anonymity, people know Sviatlana as Angelina in the branch of business where Adam works. In fact, in most places these days.

"I don't know why you don't use it more often. Boris does, most of the time."

"I prefer your real name whenever possible. Tell me about this Adam."

"He's big, almost as big as Boris. Except, no one is as big as Boris."

"Your grandad was."

Sviatlana sighs. "What I mean is, he can protect me. Against ... well, anyone."

"Well, I'm not sure who anyone might be. But unless this Adam has training and experience and is a highly skilled natural-born killer, I don't think he'd stand a chance against Boris, for example. And I think that, as another example, Boris would also lose against your father."

"Well, it would never come to that," she says, pouting a little. "But still, I like him ... and ... I want to ask him out on a date. What do you think?"

"Have you asked your father?"

"Hell, no!"

Doc smiles. "Wise choice, I think."

"Well?"

"You're a grown woman, of course. Your choices *should* be for you alone. But you know ... well, you'll need to be *extremely* careful how you handle this. He will not like it one little bit."

Sviatlana nods.

"It sounds dangerous," Boris says, puffing on his borrowed smoke.

"Yes. We'll need to watch her."

Sviatlana

Fifty years ago

"More, Sviatlana?" Val says while pouring. It's not a question. More a demand. Or a command. Vodka gushes from bottle to glass.

"Enough, Dad! We've had too much already," Sviatlana says, laughing heartily, complaining half-heartedly, trying to make herself heard above the music.

Occasionally, she misses these times with her dad. When he's at his best, he's charming, witty, caring, and even flamboyantly entertaining in a misleading, chaotic kind of way. But Val is quite the opposite of chaotic. And he's only ever at his best when they are alone together. So, it's been four years at least—since she fell in love with Adam.

"And stop using that name," she scolds. "It may only be for this evening, but if you get into bad habits, you could slip up in front of Adam one day." But Sviatlana knows her point is moot.

Nevertheless, "Call me Angelina," she says deliberately. "My name is Angelina." She tries to force some meager influence on the evening's proceedings.

Pathetic, she thinks. *Contradicting a name change you couldn't care less about.*

Sviatlana's past and future life is mostly laid out for her. So, she aims for small victories, appeasing signs of potential independence, albeit, in fact, unimaginable. Her move to marry Adam is exceptional and by far the most rebellious, and she's still not sure she'll get away with it.

Valery's documentation specialist had prepared many identities immediately after Sviatlana's birth, and Valery implemented their name changes over the decades. Their favorites are the key names they use in their underground world: Valentine, or Val, and Angelina.

Three years after Belarus finally became an EU member state, during Sviatlana's seventh year, Valentine and Angelina moved to live in Western Europe, on paper at least. The division and transfer of companies and funds from East to West took almost a decade and involved many more fake IDs. The personal and business moves to the EU removed any remaining challenges related to Val's tunneling under Ukraine and through Europe.

After more than two decades of digging and building, Valentine completed the first major phase of his underground world a few years behind schedule, one year after the conclusion of the three-year Belarus-Ukrainian revolution. The Russians had covertly sparked a synchronized upheaval in both countries, which culminated in a horrific and bloody final third year. In a rare flurry of anger, the European Parliament took the unprecedented measure of evicting Belarus from the EU, effectively forcing the country into independence once again. Ukraine was divided into East and West, the East becoming largely integrated with and controlled by Russia.

Valentine's underworld businesses had provided weapons in large numbers at ridiculous discounts to support the revolutionists: The Belarusian split from the EU was in Val's interest now he'd finished abusing EU membership to achieve his Western startup goals.

Once the dust settled, the names of Maksim and Valery were the stuff of crime-world legends; Sviatlana, they elevated to the status of mythical she-devil; Valery began to reap the benefits of his investment fully, and Valentine was content. Maximizing the opportunities created by events over three decades, Valery had neatly created a hidden world that railroaded literally from east to west, with public and secret identities and lives in both regions. Nothing could prevent him from expanding even further into Europe and Asia.

Unperturbed by his daughter-niece's mild chiding, Val presses on as if he hasn't heard her.

"Best Russian vodka money can buy. You can never have enough," he says, speaking English yet rolling his Rs and slurring in his best Russian accent, which is perfect, of course, considering his Belarusian origin. He pours a considerable measure for himself, and after handing Sviatlana her glass, he chinks their cut lead crystal tumblers together. A tiny drop of vodka splashes on his fingers. He licks it off as if sucking fresh blood from a small cut.

"And the evening is ours," he proclaims. "I've taken time off work to be with you. Your lover is halfway around the world. It's perfect." He wraps his thick arm passionately around her lower back while speaking. "Good food, good wine, then vodka, a shit hot stash, and great sex."

"Not lover, Dad. Fiancé," she says quickly, bordering on harshly.

It would have annoyed him, had he not noticed her strictly imposed self-control. He's no stranger to her temper or the effort it takes to control it.

Val says 'fiancé' sparingly, only when it's absolutely necessary. And never in private, as if his voluntary usage of the word would indicate his acceptance of their alliance, which would be incorrect.

Marriage is a subject they haven't discussed, or argued about, for a while. But she's not surprised he brings it up now they're alone. He never stops making comments. Little digs here and there to test the water, checking for cracks appearing in the unbreachable wall she'd built between them. A barrier Val once thought was impossible.

Val pulls her hips against him, and Sviatlana feels him wanting her. Placing both hands flat on his chest, she leans back and pushes him away. Gently at first, then more firmly as he resists. But she has no real chance of escaping this humongous man with the physique of a well-trained heavyweight wrestler. He must come in at forty kilos more than her.

"And I've told you, Dad, Adam and I are trying to have a baby. It'll not go down well if it turns out to be yours. So, no sex."

Val relaxes his grip slightly, and Sviatlana deftly twists her hips and slips away. Val makes a gamely display of trying to stop her, his flailing arms missing her, and he laughs. But Sviatlana sees a momentary flash of irritation course across his face, hardening the glint in his eyes.

"Don't be silly, Sveta," Val says, stubbornly using the Russian nickname and smiling meekly. "Why waste this opportunity? And I'll be careful. We'll make sure you don't get pregnant. Haven't we always?"

"Hah, that was easy after I went on The Fruit," Sviatlana scoffs.

As they still called him back then, even the great Valery didn't see the point in risking breaking the law in this area. The authorities strictly monitor the administration of The Fruit worldwide, and Valery hadn't yet obtained an illegal supply. But more importantly, The Fruit could interfere with the healthy growth of Sviatlana's reproductive system if used too early. So, from age seven, he'd secretly used a strong contraceptive which he hand-fed to the child. To be doubly sure, Doc later also placed an implant to prevent any accidental illegal conception until she started on The Fruit.

Apart from starting at a younger age, Valery showed more patience in his sexual relationship with Sviatlana and certainly more care and consideration than with Alena. He had somehow controlled himself better. He'd learned from Alena that the emotional damage could be irreparable. He forced himself to see it as Sviatlana's education. And his, for that matter. And he found that he was good at teaching. On the whole, Sviatlana responded well.

"And, *Angelina,* my dear," Val continues, again undeterred, "I have a special treat lined up for you. Some prize beauties close by. You can choose as many as you like," he says, taunting and wagging his phone.

Unlocking the screen, Val shows Angelina a live video stream from his exclusive nightclub. Hundreds of people naïvely enjoying an intimately friendly get-together. All relatively young and very pretty; some are even beautiful. Many are dancing, and most are chic yet scantily dressed—more glistening naked skin than clothing, legs entwined, groin gyrating against groin. Others sit at tables sniffing, smoking, groping, drinking, and laughing.

It's like watching a horror movie in which she will soon become the star.

Chills race up and down her back. Fear? Excitement? Angelina's body craves and begs for everything she sorely misses now she's with Adam: The thrills and releases she constantly denies herself in an attempt to lead a more normal life. And the adrenalin rush from a finely timed kill is unmatched by any drug-induced stimulant.

Val had carefully introduced Angelina to their murderous pleasure-seeking on her eighteenth birthday: His ultimate adrenalin game. Already hardened to blood and death through her combat training, Angelina had taken to the game like water off a duck's back. And she became addicted. Now, the burning urge hits harder than ever, sending her mind into an almost panic-like dash to find her release.

Then Angelina senses her father's anticipation as he watches her drooling over his bait. Her short temper boils her blood in an instant. *Get a grip! Don't let him control you!* And she shoves the phone away from her. But she feels a conflicting titillating spark as her fingers touch his hand. *Control, damn it!*

"You're making this really hard on me, Dad. But I can't. You know my relationship with Adam won't work if I go back to ..." Angelina struggles to find a word for this heinous pastime they've perfected over the past two decades. She cannot. How many have they slaughtered? She's uncertain she could count them if she wanted. "... back to this," she finishes quietly, indicating his phone with a thrust of her chin.

"Milashka, don't be so hard on yourself," he says gently, warmly. He reaches out, grasps her by the shoulder, then slides his hand slowly up to the back of her neck, caressing lovingly. "We both know our needs are beyond average, and your boy-man wouldn't even begin to understand them, let alone satisfy you."

"He's fifty-one, Dad. He's not a boy," she says, protesting in Adam's defense, not for the first time. But *she* knows it's true. Adam cannot bring her to any kind of peak or climax although, god forbid, Adam doesn't know that.

Angelina never really expected to find any normal person who could satisfy her. But it's a price she'd agreed with herself that she'd pay. Maybe it was even part of being normal. Who knows? But at the time, she'd thought it was a small sacrifice. Happiness comes in many forms, doesn't it?

"He's weak, like a boy, and he'll never grow strong. It's already too late for that," Val argues abruptly and shakes his head.

She doesn't *want* to rile him further. But she shares her father's genes. Angelina turns away from her father, hiding her expression.

"Just because he's not a murderous fucking psychopath doesn't mean he's not a ma ..." she yells. *Control!* she thinks, too late.

Still amazingly fast considering his age, Val has moved swiftly up behind her and reaches Angelina even before she finishes her sentence. He wraps an arm around and across the front of her hips, pulling her close. With the other hand, he reaches forward and squeezes and pulls on her breasts, working her top down, lower and lower. Angelina knows he'll not relinquish this hold willingly.

"*Not* being something doesn't qualify his manhood," Val says, his tone a quiet growl.

Angelina tries to pull away, but he tightens his grip and presses his hips hard against her backside.

He's lost his patience quickly this evening, she thinks. *Four years' abstinence has left him hu ...*

"Something like this," he says, pulling back and thrusting himself against her buttocks again so violently that her head flicks back, "could prove his manhood. But I'll wager his wouldn't work when you needed it most."

"Oh, you'd be surpri ..."

"I ... don't ... like ... surprises," he says, dry humping her fiercely to punctuate each word, his grip on her becoming painful, each push bringing them closer to a nearby sofa. And he's all-the-way angry and aroused.

No going back now. She knows he'll try not to hurt her. That he'll be sorry afterward. And that's the best Angelina can expect from this evening: an apology. The rest will get ugly.

She'll be sorry herself later. She can already feel the monster in her rising. Her plans for a normal life must wait. And it's her own fault. She brought this on herself, didn't she? She's thirty-eight years old and the complete opposite of stupid. She should have seen this coming, avoided it. *Why didn't I?*

I didn't want to, Angelina thinks, confused and conflicted.

Part of her needs a break, a fix, some release from the struggle of this craving-creating self-control. And she needs to kill. But part of her wants to tuck herself up in bed, head under the covers, and cry. *Why is my life like this? How did I get this messed up? Why couldn't I have a normal father and mother? A regular life? What's all this good for?*

Angelina squeezes her eyes closed and imagines herself curled in a ball on the floor in the corner of the massive old-fashioned room. She can even smell the musky stench of the dust-ridden century-old carpet; she's escaped down there many times before.

Inwardly, she whimpers about things she never had and misses like a hole where her heart ought to be, shedding tears of suffering from so many moments she tries so hard not to remember. Angelina wails in silent agony as a hellish fire fills the gaping void in her chest, torturing and driving her toward more pain for pain's sake in a vicious circle of distraction.

It shouldn't be fire, she thinks vaguely, uncertain of how it should feel. Alone and scared in the old room, Angelina weeps some more until Val places his heavy hand on her shoulder and squeezes hard. A massive pain shoots through her, and she throws her head back, gasps, and cries out. It's an all too familiar feeling, though, and she can't help but welcome it, revel in it, knowing where it will take her. She can relate to it and control it. And explore it.

Angelina's ripped thong lies on the carpet. Compromised, forced forward over the back of the sofa, Angelina's father has pinned her down from behind. He slams into her, hips smacking against buttocks, her short, pressed-out shrieks coaxing him on further. With each thrust, he hammers her self-esteem deeper into its eternal burial place, but she becomes stronger, and harder. Or so she tells herself.

"Forget what I said about being careful. That wasn't a serious offer," he taunts.

Yet he's somehow also tender. *Loving, isn't he?*

Val pauses and pulls a slim remote from his shirt pocket. With one press of a button, a hovering table stacked with goodies floats to within comfortable reach for Angelina. Without thinking, she submits and snorts the closest two rows of powder.

The first rush hits her fast, and she closes her eyes, smiles widely, and with her whole body, she mocks the world. *You want me? Well, now you got me!* She squeezes, pushes her hips backward, and twists down hard on him.

His turn to suffer a little. And slowly, she turns his pain into her pleasure.

"Argh," he gasps quietly. But he, too, is no stranger to pain and turns it to his advantage.

"You've been mine since before you were born," he almost croons, smiling, plunging into her. "And you'll be mine long after I'm dead." Jabbing hard. *And your brats will be mine.* Stabbing deep.

"No one could ever love you like I do," Val whispers. *And no one ever will,* he promises.

Angelina hears a new noise and opens her eyes. A young man stands before her, well built, scantily dressed, and skin finely glistening. He drops his pants and then steps onto the sofa close to her.

He'll be a challenge in more ways than one, Angelina thinks and smiles to herself while reaching her hand out to him.

Val guides his daughter's other arm behind a sofa cushion, and she shivers at the touch of the hidden blade's smooth grip. Angelina knows exactly which knife it is. Her years of combat training have given her intimate knowledge and expertise with many deadly weapons.

That should do the job, she figures, and hurls herself into her favorite game.

FUTILE FIX

"Where's Adam?" Val demands, stepping out from behind his bureau.

"I'm so sorry, Dad," Angelina says, palms outraised. "Some crisis at work. He called me last minute to say he'd be late. Said I should come over and pour you one on his expense account."

"Damn it, I make a special effort to be nice, and he can't even be on time!" Val says.

"I'm really, really sorry."

"OK, OK. I guess I shouldn't complain. It's usually me blowing off appointments," Val says, smiling and raising *his* palms apologetically, and he wraps his other arm around her shoulder. "Let's go to the drawing room, and you can follow your fiancé's instructions. But you'd better make it a good one," he says and laughs.

Wow, easier than expected, Angelina thinks. *He even said the F word.* She keeps a watchful eye on which path her dad takes through the house. Three months earlier, he held the evening's entertainment in a part of the old mansion they don't use often, and it ended badly. But the usual short walk to the main lounge sets her at ease, and she crosses over to the bar to prepare the drinks. She doesn't ask. He prefers whisky before dinner.

Val loves that his daughter cares enough to know his preferences. Angelina smiles on seeing he's put out a bottle of her favorite Russian Beluga. She doesn't seem to notice that there's no other vodka on offer this evening.

Chinking their heavy glasses together, Val says, "Let's hope that man of yours gets here soon. I'm hungry."

"I can call him. That might help," she says.

"No need. Let him do what he needs to."

They knock back the opening round together. The first one always goes down fast.

"Let me do the honors this time," Val says categorically, taking her glass, and she sits back while he pours for them. "Do you know what was so urgent?"

"He's been working a high-profile case, and there's been a breakthrough. I don't know more. All classified stuff," Angelina says as she takes the refilled tumbler from him, immediately taking a large gulp.

Val puts up a show of mock disgust. "Well, that's not good. No matter who told me I should, I'd never keep any secrets from you."

"Hah," Angelina scoffs. "You have a million secrets. And besides, you'd probably fire him if he told me."

"Never!" Val says, loud and laughing, and then he reaches out his arm as Angelina's eyes glaze over. The solid crystal glass bounces on the thick carpet, the vodka spraying through the air, and Val catches Angelina as she falls. He carries her over to a comfy chair prepared specially for the occasion.

She'd not noticed that, either. Missed the vodka and the easy chairs. Getting sloppy, he thinks. *She should've suspected something when I was so laid back about him being late.*

And the ungrateful bitch went for the liquor as I suspected. Even in her condition. Tried for over two years to get pregnant, then when I do the honors, she doesn't care about the kid? What if it's his?

Val's not sure why Angelina's so confident her pregnancy is because of that night three months ago. But he's not worried.

It doesn't matter either way. All contingencies are prepared for, Val thinks. *The DNA test will tell.* Prenatal paternity tests are one hundred percent accurate these days. And fast. *Modern medicine,* he smiles to himself.

But why hasn't she told Adam? Val presses a button on the computer installed in the bar, and before his third whisky is poured, Doc arrives with a hovering hospital bed, his bag, and some equipment lying on top.

"Are you sure you want to keep her sedated? I *have* mentioned the minor risk of deformity and the even smaller chance of the child not surviving, haven't I?" Doc double-checks, clearly reluctant.

"Let's get on with it, Doc. We've been through this already," Val says, and they lift Angelina onto the bed. Val takes out his phone and starts typing a message.

"OK. Let's get this test started," Doc says, collecting a blood sample and popping it into a DNA testing machine attached to the end of the bed. He administers a drip containing nutrients, The Fruit, and enough sedative to keep Angelina asleep for forty-eight hours. "That should do it," he says.

Looking up from his mobile, Val says, "Thanks, Doc. You take it from here. Anything I should know?"

Doc shakes his head. "You can check the monitor when you're not busy," he says, indicating Val's phone with his head. "But I'll stay close to her."

Escorting the old medic to the door, Val says, "Call me *as soon* as you have the result, Doc. I want to know if I'm going to be a granddad." *Or not.*

But Doc's not convinced. *Does he really expect her to keep it if it's his? This will not end well,* he thinks, and he drags his feet while trundling back to his lab with Angelina.

Sprawled back on the drawing room sofa, enjoying his whisky and speculating on the DNA result, Val takes comfort in knowing his daughter is sleeping, safely locked away. *But no matter what,* he thinks, *she'll be mine again soon. And I'll avoid two disasters with one blow, or in one evening.* Val smiles as if he'd just whispered "Cheers" to the devil.

But something's been nagging at the back of Val's mind these past weeks, and now it surfaces again and damn near tugs him from his perch. But he still can't put his finger on it.

Val forces himself to think through recent conversations, analyzing, searching for the trigger. It doesn't take long.

It's Doc, Val thinks. Doc's concern about Angelina's sedation remains fresh in Val's mind. *I've seen that look on him before. He doesn't like it. Of course he doesn't. But why's that a problem? I knew he wouldn't like it. Hell, I don't like it, but what choice do I have?* She *was the one who fell for Adam. She wasn't supposed to do that.*

So, now I need to fix it. ... Ahhh. ... And there it is. Impossible to fix. She's screwed with my master plan, and I'm desperately trying to save it.

Val gets up for a refill. *But it's sabotaged, destroyed, and like a fool, I've been hanging on, hoping.*

Val sits down with his refill. *Damn it, I can't win,* he thinks. *Got to cut my losses. Limit the damage.*

Sipping on his liquor, Val swallows the brutal truths he realizes he's avoided for too long. Then he makes a call. Doc answers immediately.

"Change of plan, Doc. Get rid of the brat. Tonight. Right now," Val says and hangs up, not wanting a response. His next call is to another employee. "Plan B, Susan," he says, ending the call and sitting back to finish his drink. He closes his eyes and prepares himself.

Val's vibrating phone jolts him from a short power nap, the colorful screen showing Adam's face. His prospective son-in-law is a high-flying lawyer employed by his own organization. That's how Adam met Angelina, which only compounds Val's frustration. Val has often thought it would be simple to dispose of Adam, but just as frequently felt that Angelina would guess the obvious and never forgive him. Besides, he'd lose his only inside source of information. While Val hasn't heard much from Adam over the years, it has been far more than from his close-lipped daughter.

"What's up, Adam?"

"Can you talk?" Whispering.

Ridiculous idiot. "Yes, I can," Val says. He stands and begins walking to the door. "Your lover-girl is comatose. Have you guys been overdoing it? She's exhausted. Had one stiff drink and then crashed on the sofa. I told her dinner could wait and to go and sleep." *I could have had a career on stage,* Val thinks.

"She's working too hard, Dad," Adam answers.

"Dad" cringes. *Not a chance.* "So, what *is* up?" Val asks again.

"This is not working out. Someone bought up all the rooms in the hotel I wanted. For a whole month!"

Val smiles.

"They've refunded my booking. On top of that, the crisis in the Congo threatens to escalate imminently into a full-blown civil war. So, civilian travel requires government approval. Our chance of getting in is almost zero. Do you have any idea how disappointed she'll be?" Adam says.

Val says, "The Congo? You didn't mention going into a war zone."

"I thought you knew she'd set her heart on honeymooning there. And I don't think she'll let a little war stop her," Adam explains. "But I wanted to surprise her."

"Hmmm," Val muses. "We'll need to make sure she's safe. Look, there's always a solution. We just need to find it. She's fast asleep now. I'll come over, and we can brainstorm. I already have some ideas," Val offers. "Forward her number to me; I'll handle her if she happens to wake, which she won't," he says convincingly and hangs up the call, not leaving time for Adam to object.

Minutes later, Val's standing in one of his offices on the fourteenth floor, shaking Adams' hand.

"That was fast, Dad," Adam says, astonished.

"I always have a driver ready," Val lies. *Wouldn't be a secret if I told everyone, would it now?* Val smiles to himself.

Thirty-nine years ago, Val chose a location in Ukraine as the center of his secret underground enterprise, mainly because it's not far but is also a safe distance from his homeland and his family's traditional mansion. The property has been in his family for more than a hundred and fifty years. Val buried his parents and grandparents in the adjacent graveyard, which is, unbeknown to most, also part of the family's estate; Val was born there and has lived in the mansion his whole life, and he cherishes the place dearly.

Val's subterranean project's initial roaring success secured the immediate continuation of the second major phase, which included expansion into Belarus, Lithuania, Latvia, and Russia and added to Val's many private tunnels. The route he uses most travels from Ukraine to Belarus, passing under his home and office buildings.

Unlike his other subterranean settlements, Val didn't plan any industrial or other significant business activities close to his home. But five more years' construction saw the completion of various luxurious entertainment complexes spread under his mansion and over to the offices, all connected with super-fast elevators and transport corridors, most of which Val reserves solely for his use.

Val's underworld plans include a great number of such entertainment facilities. Many are already operational. Anyone with enough money and nerve can book anything from an out-of-this-world evening dinner to an unlimited stay in these opulent, high-security, oasis-like adult fun parks designed for the usually good, the bad, and the ugly alike.

Numerous high-profile criminals have as good as emigrated to Val's hidden world, much like seeking asylum. Val handles any crimes committed against his underground rules using immediate and harsh measures, with Val and his Serpents acting as jury, judge, and executioner.

The cost and, indeed, the need for silence between the empire below and the world above is extortionate and exacting. But the silence is absolute.

"Now, where's this hotel?" the future father-in-law says, getting right down to business.

Adam displays a map on the large screen. A marker points to Pointe-Noir in the Congo.

"Great place. Been there numerous times."

"You have?" Adam asks, surprised.

"Why do you think she wants to go there? She's seen the pictures. Fell in love with the place. Which hotel?"

Adam clicks on the marker.

"Congo Palace, huh? Not bad. Pricey, for sure, but right on the beach. Who bought it out?"

And so, they talk through the details of the honeymoon trip. Adam waits patiently while "Dad" makes one phone call after another.

"The president will be free in an hour," Val says finally, hanging up, and Adam raises his eyebrows. "What say you to a drink while we wait?" Val slaps Adam gently but firmly on the shoulder, then he turns and walks away. Adam runs to catch up.

"What if Sleeping Beauty wakes up?" Adam says.

"I just had the maid look in on her. Still out for the count. Did you forward her calls?" Val asks, leading Adam into an elevator.

"Damn, no, hang on." Adam grabs his phone and starts work on it. When he raises his eyes again, the elevator doors and Adam's mouth open in unison. They look out into a massive multi-roomed luxury club that Adam's never seen before. Only a select few phones can send the elevator down this far.

The vast space loosely divides into a dining area to the right, tables all set for dinner, many occupied; a large relaxation bay surrounded by floor-to-ceiling smart-glass dividers filled with sofas, coffee tables, comfy chairs, and a gaming area sports several gambling tables. To the left is a dance floor with high round pub tables and tall stools around the walls. Down one side wall, different-sized booths offer a little more privacy.

Special acoustics techniques and the glass walls confine the loud music to the dance area. If you look carefully, discretely placed doors and open corridors blend in around the walls as if camouflaged, some providing entry to the guests, others leading off to who-knows-where. In a dividing line down the center of the club, a vast oval, glistening black marble bar displays the complete collection of drinks available on the planet, so it seems. Hundreds of young adults enjoy the many activities the private club offers. None look above thirty years old, and all dressed like fashion models in a show.

"Oh wow! I didn't know this place was here," Adam says.

"It's private. Let's sit over here," Val says, leading the way to a sofa. "What will you drink? Whisky? Bourbon? Vodka?"

"I could fancy a good Russian vodka—like you have at home. Do they have it here?" Adam answers, gazing at the bar.

"Of course. Relax, and I'll get some." Val smiles broadly, then turns away to avoid suppressing his excitement. He wants to enjoy this feeling. *This couldn't have gone better if I'd spent a thousand hours planning it!* Val thinks.

In Val's very own flamboyant style, he practically flings the tumblers onto the table in front of Adam, then drops down beside him, picks up his own glass, raises it, and waits. Adam rushes to grab his vodka, and they chink glasses together.

"So, what do you think?" Val asks, surveying the club.

"Absolutely fantastic," Adam says, smiling and looking around as if he were a teenager again.

Val takes two large gulps, and his whisky disappears. Adam watches, then follows suit.

"That first one always disappears fast," Val says. "Let me arrange another; then I'll give you a tour." And again, not waiting for Adam, Val returns to the bar, a cocksure smile set on his face.

As the girl behind the bar hands him new tumblers, Val slips another tiny pill into Adam's vodka. *Two should do the trick,* he thinks.

Back at the sofa and grinning at Adam, Val holds out the vodka. *Get off your ass, boy. Come and get it.*

Val studies Adam's movements as he pulls himself to his feet. *Five to ten more minutes*, he guesses. *Time for a quick walk about.*

"This kitchen has some of the finest chefs in the world," Val says as they reach the dining area. He hands Adam a menu. "It changes every day. But you can order whatever you want if you have enough money and time to wait. This fish comes from ..." Val continues wandering the club, boasting about this and that. Anything really, to fill the time while constantly observing Adam.

Eventually, while passing by the row of tables down one side of the dance floor, Val stops. "Everything all right, Adam?"

"What? Oh, yes. Is it me, or are many of these people practically naked?" Adam asks, doing his best not to stare.

"Ah, I see," Val says, and he smiles back knowingly, nodding, and rests his glass on one of the high pub tables.

They stand for a moment while Adam enjoys the view.

Val also pretends to scan the room but rarely takes his eyes off Adam. *Always interesting to see which kicks in first. Looks like lover boy here has already got it up.*

Val had spiked Adam's drinks at the bar with Doc's carefully blended concoction of aphrodisiac, stimulant, opiate, and hallucinogen. It was a complicated process, creating a mix that gave each drug its chance to work, complimenting the others instead of conflicting.

Years and millions to develop that cocktail. But my god, it was worth it. The drug has ranked among his top five sellers for almost three decades.

"It's enough to tempt even the strongest," Val says. "One could easily spend the whole evening here with an inconsolable erection. Or one could do something about it," he laughs loudly. "Look at her!" Val says. "Wouldn't mind getting my hands on that."

"Hell yeah," Adam responds, a little too fast.

"Come on, let's take a look over there," Val says as he picks up his glass. He glances back quickly to check Adam is following.

The room lighting behind the door in the wall is dimmer than the main club area. Two girls and two guys lounge around a table in the room's center. One guy stretches across from the sofa to the table, elbows supporting him as he snorts a line of white powder. Then he looks up as the newcomers get closer.

"Hey, man, come on in. There's plenty to go round," the guy says.

Get your god-damned shoes off my fucking sofa, you good-for-nothing punk. "Yeah, I know; they're mine," Val says, smiling a little sternly.

"Er, I'm Jimmy, that's Chelsea, Susan's the blonde wonder over there, and that's Watson."

"Yeah. I know that too," Val says.

"Great place you got here, man," Watson proclaims, looking around approvingly as if surveying the entire club through the walls.

"Thanks. I like it," Val says, grinning. "Glad you're enjoying yourselves." He continues to smile to put them at ease. Glancing over the tumblers on the table, he picks out a pill.

"Aphrodisiac," he explains to Adam, holding it between two fingers. "In case I feel like a little fun myself. Man my age can use a little boost to help with that extra mile or two," he chuckles, then knocks the pill back with a swig of whisky.

"But *you* don't need that, I see," says Susan, the blonde. She walks over to Adam and grabs him firmly yet carefully with one hand, rubbing up and down. "You're all ready for this, aren't you, lover boy?" she teases.

Adam glances over to his future father-in-law, but Val raises a palm towards him, and smiling, he turns and walks over to Chelsea. He wraps his arm around her waist, pulls her hips against his, and kisses her gently.

"What do you guys say we go somewhere even more private?" Val says.

Jimmy looks longingly at the drugs on the table. "Can we take this stuff with us?"

"Hah, there's plenty more where we're going," Val says, barking a short laugh and pointing. A door in a far wall opens automatically.

Val moves alongside Adam as they enter the new room. He sees Adam's pants, already unzipped. *Oh, she's so damned good at this. One of my best investments.*

"You can have anyone you want," Val tells Adam discreetly while following the others. The door clicks quietly as it locks automatically behind them. "I prefer two at a time. You OK with three and three?" he asks.

"Er, er ..." Adam stumbles.

"That's a deal then," Val chuckles. "What's it gonna be, at least for the first round? Girl? Boy? That Watson looks like a fine catch if you ask me?"

"Er, yeah. I was thinking that too," Adam says, his cheeks red.

Susan stays close to Adam, walking beside him, still working the front of his pants, keen to take it to the next level. Watson, Chelsea, and Jimmy gravitate to the low center table where the drugs are ready.

"Why don't you start with Watson? Susan will fill in where it's needed. I'll take the other two. OK?" Val presses on while looking at Susan.

She nods once.

"Sure," Adam says, unable to suppress a smile.

So much for a monogamous bloody marriage, you two-timing dick-for-a-brain. Val thinks. *Can't wait to show this to my girl.*

"Come on then, Adam," Susan says, her voice low and humming. "Let's get you warmed up with Watson. I'll decide what I want once you've chosen what you want. If you need any help, give me a sign." She leads Adam over to pull Watson apart from the group.

Not his first time, Susan thinks as she observes Adam place his hands on Watson's hips and deftly twist him into a kiss.

In no time at all, most of them have discarded their clothing, and the scene displays the beginnings of a bona fide orgy.

Val mentally steps back for a moment, elevates his thoughts, and visualizes what's happening. He studies the position of the players and runs over the plan. He sees the big shining blades under the sofa within easy reach for Susan, safely concealed behind and under cushions on the couch but easily accessible if you know they're there.

Two rounds, if the first one is clean. Val imagines the possible progression of the players' movements and how the first round could end. *Yes. With a bit of luck, this could go very well.*

Doc mutes the volume and swivels his stool away from the screen. Val's kind of fun is not for him. Besides, he has work to finish.

He observes Angelina as she lies peacefully in bed. Like a researcher, he studies her. Not with his eyes but with his mind. He tries to be her, to imagine her reaction, thoughts, and feelings when she hears the news of what has happened. But he cannot.

Doc believes he can empathize with people in an entirely unique manner. He learns someone's personality traits, then imposes that person's role upon himself absolutely, thus temporarily modifying his own character. And in assuming the position of the other, both in a cognitive and emotional sense, he feels what they might feel, and even thinks what they might think. He suspects this gift is possible because he has no heart or conscience. Nothing binds him to one life or another, and very likely, he's even missing a soul.

However, when it comes to Angelina, he simply cannot impose her character on himself. Whenever he tries to understand Angelina, to get inside her mind, Alena steps in and takes control of him.

So, Alena studies her daughter, suffers with her baby girl, and is angry, hateful, and vengeful on Sviatlana's behalf. And as Alena painstakingly empathizes with her child, she promises to care for her, take her revenge, and kill that bastard who hurts and kills so many. Alena's emotions are so ferocious she threatens to overrule Doc's consciousness forever, and he has to fight his way back to master his own destiny, ridding himself of this bitter, angry dead mother.

I must be going mad, he thinks. He squeezes his eyes tightly, rubbing them slowly and hard, recovering, or resurfacing, until after a while, he's ready to continue clearing away the last signs of the removal of Angelina's fetus. Then he kisses Angelina's forehead, his lips barely brushing her skin, and he rechecks her drip before guiding a hovering desk out into the corridor to his private lounge as he jokingly thinks of it. And there he waits for Val to call him.

Laid back on the sofa, feet up on the low table before him and well into his second large vodka, Doc's head jerks abruptly, and he tightens his grasp on his glass to save it from falling. After dry-washing his face with his free hand, he sits up and turns when, from the corner of his eye, he notices some unusual movement on his computer screen. His eyebrows pull together as he studies the lay of the land.

Something's wrong!

Almost everyone in the room appears to be dead, but that's not the problem. Doc turns up the volume, and after a few more seconds, he slams his glass down hard on the table and dashes from the room while struggling to pull out his phone.

"What the fuck?" Adam says, looking around him, eyes darting here and there, a medium-sized Bowie knife clenched in his fingers. Blood seeps from a thin, diagonal red line across his belly. Watson's lying face down, not far from the sofa, a large pool of blood under his abdomen and hips. *Dead?*

Susan is sprawled on the floor on the other side of the couch. Adam knows she's dead; he killed her himself. *Self-defense,* he thinks. He shakes his head, trying to master his confusion, then looks over at Val, who's sitting up, somewhat surprised and trying to work out what's gone wrong.

Pulling himself into a more upright position, Val leans his arm heavily on the back of the sofa, flat and bent at the elbow, his closed fist wrapped around a huge knife, its tip pointing at the ceiling. The knife handle's base digs into the cushion; bright red blood drips from the blade and down over the hilt onto Val's fingers. Chelsea's arm and head hang over one end of the sofa, fingertips almost touching the floor, her mass of brunette curls covering her features.

"You bastard!" Adam cries out as he raises his arm high and begins to charge over to Val.

Val grunts as he springs to his feet and over the back of the sofa, but as fast as he is, the gap between them is small, and there's no time to gain a firm stance. Adam attacks, bringing his knife down in a ferocious but uncontrolled strike aimed at Val's neck.

Val blocks Adam's arm, but it's too late, too slow, and the angle's all wrong. Adam's blade sinks into Val's upper chest below his left shoulder. No stranger to pain, Val ignores the wound and the knife sticking out of him, and without a moment's hesitation, he swings his much longer blade up into the front of Adam's neck at the back of the jaw and into his brain. Then he pulls his knife free, chucks it behind him, and shoves Adam to the floor.

Little shit had more in him than I expected.

Glancing briefly at the knife sticking from his chest, Val walks slowly over to the bar, pours a large vodka, and rests a supporting palm on the smooth marble surface as he drinks. Then he steps over to Susan, looks down at her, and pokes her neck with his toes. *Dead as a dodo, poor cow. I'm gonna miss her.*

On a bookshelf built into the wall on the far side of the room, Val finds and presses a hidden button just as Boris bursts in with security guards and Doc hot on his tail. Some of Boris's Serpents, dressed in plastic, are ready to clean up.

"That was fast!" Val says and laughs, but even that hurts, so he groans instead.

"I decided to check on you," Doc says. "And saw things were going wrong."

Val nods appreciatively, then unwraps his index finger from around his glass and points at the knife. "Take a look at this, will you."

Doc glances at the blade protruding from Val's lower shoulder. "We must go to my theater to deal with this," he says and escorts Val from the room, leaving the Serpents to their task.

ACTION ...

My very own Sleeping Beauty, Val thinks and sighs silently while staring down at his drugged, unconscious daughter-niece. He wallows in pride as if he alone had conceived and perfected the concept of selective reproduction and, thus, had single-handedly crafted this miracle.

The westward-falling sun's fiery rays shining through the window burn orange streaks in Angelina's copper-red hair and surround her face in a gentle golden-red glow. The very vision of an angel.

Enough to capture anyone's heart. Val smiles and sighs quietly. But then he explodes within. *Especially when they get a sense of how much she's worth! Take Adam: Exhibit A!*

But she's mine, Val tells himself fiercely. Then, forcing himself to calm down, he takes one of her hands in his and absentmindedly strokes the back with his other hand. *She'll always be mine.*

"How's your shoulder?" Doc asks, entering and joining Val at the bedside.

"It's fine," Val says and grimaces. "The drugs help. But I need the movement back as fast as possible," he complains. In Val's profession, such a disabling injury is a vulnerability, despite his security measures, because even the fiercest loyalty can only suffer so much.

"It hasn't been two days yet, Val. Weeks more, maybe months, remember? And don't forget, keep as still as possible at first. That's the fastest track to recovery," Doc says, repeating an earlier warning.

"Fifteen minutes to wake up after you inject her, correct?" Val asks, his words short and crisp.

"Correct."

"We should bind her down," Val says. "I don't want to go grappling with her in my condition. And she'll get upset when she sees ..."

"You're going to show her?" Doc says, raising his eyebrows.

"Yes. I'll show her that he wasn't any better than the rest of us. That she was in love with him for all the wrong reasons." Val's voice becomes louder and harsher as he speaks.

"Does love need a reason? On the contrary, surely?" Doc challenges gently, trying not to provoke him further.

Val has never physically hurt Doc, but he's been angry with him numerous times, furious sometimes to the point of threatening violence. But Val respects Doc in his own way. More importantly, he needs him. Probably too much, and

Doc knows it. Nevertheless, Doc is always careful.

"Sure as hell does. But I won't discuss this now. Bind her and give her the wake-up shot. I'll be back soon," Val says and leaves the room.

Surely, he realizes the risk he's taking? Doc thinks, staring at Angelina. But then Val returns, holding a glass of whisky.

"Is it done?" Val asks.

Doc nods as he answers. "She'll wake within minutes. Do you want me to wait with you?"

"In the other room. Just in case."

"Hit this button if she needs sedating again. It's milder, but she'll sleep fast enough," Doc says, pointing to the first in a row of green buttons on the side of a medical trolley. Multiple drip cables lead into one cannula, secured into Angelina's arm. The red button is to call Doc in.

"Thanks, Doc," Val says, not taking his eyes off his daughter.

As Doc leaves, Val retrieves a remote from a wall-side cupboard and presses a few buttons. A Nu-Li-Aerially-powered hovering screen floats from the ceiling to the end of Angelina's bed.

A minute later, she stirs. Val bends over her slowly and kisses her gently on the cheek, grimacing from the pain in his shoulder. He rests there, close to her, until she speaks.

"Dad?" she murmurs. "What happened?"

"You don't remember?" he asks.

"No."

"Think. You must try and remember," Val instructs her, then strokes her cheek and straightens up, grimacing again.

"Just ... having a drink with you before dinner. That's all," Angelina says after a short pause.

"Hmmm. Doc said you might not remember. That you might lock away the memory of what happened. Maybe even as far back as the last happy moment you experienced. You don't remember me showing you a video?" he prompts.

"Nothing, Dad," she answers quickly. "What's happened?" She tries to sit up but feels then sees the bindings wrapped around her. "Why am I tied down?" she asks, almost panicking.

"I've tried to wake you twice, but you lost it. Screaming, kicking, trying to hurt me," Val says.

"Why would I do that?" Angelina asks, her voice cracking, the pitch rising.

"I'll show you again if you want," Val says. "But be warned, you won't like it. You didn't the last time. It ends badly," he says, and studying her face, he strokes her cheek with his knuckles.

Angelina turns her head away from his hand, eyes glaring dead ahead. She thrusts her chin at the screen, then waits, staring.

Val starts the video.

Adam trails close behind Susan, their fingertips hooked together as Susan stretches out her free hand to tease Watson into forming their trio. Angelina's body stiffens instantly, and her face turns to stone as she recognizes the room. She's seen a few videos of herself recorded there.

The first moments flick from camera to camera, showing the whole sordid scene from various positions. More than a hundred cams capture different heights and angles, and Val has edited the mini movie, showing the evolving story to suit his needs.

Lying strapped to her bed, Angelina clenches her fists, fingernails digging into her palms to help maintain self-control. But she can't stop the escaping wayward tear when it drips down her face as she watches her fiancé fucking a man, being unfaithful, on top of a blatant lie.

Adam had vehemently defended his heterosexuality once when Angelina had admitted her attraction to both sexes. "Strictly women," he'd declared like it was something to be proud of.

Val briefly pauses the video when Susan pulls her knife out from behind the cushions, ready to attack Adam.

"She should *not* have done that!" he says, pretending to still be shocked. Then he resumes playing the video. Val's been careful to include shots showing he can't see what's happening with Susan and Adam. And he's thanked his lucky stars numerous times since then that things had worked out that way. It made his case for innocence that much stronger.

"I swear I didn't mean for this to happen, Angel," Val says softly. "Susan went totally against my instructions. Probably the drugs. And Adam snapped. Tried to kill me. I've seen that look in a man's eyes before. I guess he thought it was all my doing. But I didn't want this."

"And you said he wasn't a man," Angelina says quietly, her voice grating like a scrap metal pipe scraping down a brick wall.

"Maybe I was wrong about that part. But your marriage would never have survived," Val shoots back angrily.

Angelina goes cold from within, as if some calamitous force within her rips her heart from her soul, smashes them to a thousand pieces, torches the fragments, and then pisses on the ashes to be sure there's neither fire of love nor life left in her. She closes her eyes and slowly and deliberately turns away from her father.

Val presses the green button, and within moments, Angelina feels herself drifting.

This'll be the only thing you'll remember to regret while you die, you heinous bastard, Angelina silently promises as she falls away.

... And Reaction

Soft sunlight catches Angelina's hand as she reaches out and ever so gently grasps Doc's wrist. He lays aside the final strap that had held her down.

"Will you stay with me a while?" Angelina asks. Calmer now, she's almost her usual self except for a profound sadness pressing down on her so heavily it's like a natural constraint that makes her bindings appear to have been needless.

The loss is hard on her, understandably. All her loved ones in a single fell blow. She's all alone now, Doc her only companion.

"Of course, my dear," he says, taking her hand in his.

Leaning toward his screen for a moment, Val follows carefully. He's not concerned about Doc. Unlike his bond with Alena, Doc's not emotionally close to Angelina. He cares for her, certainly, and has taken good care of her, but that's all. And although Val believes Angelina sees Doc as a kind of friend, she's not close to anyone except Val. Or that's how it used to be.

Before Adam, Val was confident that Angelina was all his. But now she's lost Adam, and Val has lost her.

No, Val's not worried about Doc. It's Angelina that Val studies, as if something important is about to escape him. Like a cat that crouches, watching for giveaway signs, ready to pounce on the escaped mouse, he waits for the chance to win her back.

On the surface, she appears fine. But Val knows that underneath her silky-smooth exterior, there broils a cauldron of complex emotions and thoughts that don't even attempt to surface. She's trained her self-control to perfection, so he only catches her true feelings in a rare momentary lapse of concentration.

I might as well not watch, Val decides. *If nothing is wrong, I'll see nothing. If there is something wrong, I'll still see nothing.* But he can't tear himself away from the screen.

Angelina rests her head on Doc's shoulder, lips brushing his ear.

Deliberate? Val asks himself. *No camera there to see her face. Does she know that? Can't remember.* He zooms in closer and turns up the volume.

"Nine days, nine hundred," Angelina whispers directly into Doc's ear, lips unmoving.

Despite Val's careful vigil, he hears nothing and can't bring her closer, no matter how hard he wishes it. She's further away from him than he could ever realize.

Nine days later, at oh-nine-hundred hours, Angelina meets Doc in the garden of a mid-town shopping complex, at a bar just inside the entrance. They order coffee to go.

It's not their first secret meeting here at Angelina's request. Under the ruse of sharing an interest in botany, they've convened a few times in this ostentatious members-only greenhouse-garden-cum-coffeehouse-cum-restaurant, annexed off the shopping complex.

Doc mostly lends a listening ear, and that covers much of what she needs. He never shares information about her father but remains loyal to Val to a fault, not out of any sense of commitment or obligation, but rather, more conscious of his personal safety—and Angelina's.

Val's aware of the visits, and Doc tells him much of what they discuss, but nothing that'll bring harm to Angelina. "Once in a while, she needs someone to talk with who she can trust," Doc explained one day to Val. "Best it's someone who won't use anything she says against you."

Val accepted that as reasonable.

Wandering the pathways silently at first, Doc studies Angelina. Making small talk and examining the flora while walking, she pauses and points at a rare African flame lily.

"Look. It's one of my favorites. Beautiful, yet deadly in the right hands." She takes a breath as if planning to continue but then pauses and quietly sighs.

"Appealing, indeed," Doc replies, and Angelina glances at him.

She seems less angry, he thinks as they resume their ambling.

"He meant well," Angelina says quietly, out of the blue, as if hearing Doc's thoughts. "Or so he says."

Can she have forgiven him? Incredulous, he questions her with a look.

"I've been talking with him these past few days. He's tried to make me understand that he meant only good for me. And even though his plan went wrong, it was accidental," she concludes.

"I see," replies Doc. "Well, I'm certain things didn't go as he expected."

"What? You mean getting stabbed in the shoulder?" Angelina asks in a low tone, glaring.

The hairs on Doc's arms rise. "That, for sure," he says with a sheepish half-smile on his downcast face.

The array of exotic blooms seems endless.

"Quite a coincidence, though—my miscarriage right at the same time, wouldn't you say?" Angelina asks him, looking him directly in the eye.

She knows something, he thinks. He doesn't respond at first but looks away, casually hooks her arm in his, and starts walking again.

She's patient, and she waits. His gut tells him she'll wait until the shopping mall closes and longer.

"Fate or fluke, the cha …"

"Fluke?" She cuts him off quickly, tone sharp as a freshly honed knife.

"Sorry, bad choice of words, my dear. More than eighty percent of miscarriages happen in the first trimester. It's estimated …"

"Don't treat me like a fool, Doc! And don't try to hide lies behind statistics," she says, spitting out her words.

He stops in his tracks and looks at her. Angelina searches his face. But Doc has decades of practice, and she sees nothing.

Damn. Confronted him too fast, she thinks.

Doc's no fool, however. And while she saw nothing, he saw plenty. He lowers his gaze, then crosses the path to a bench where he sits, and a sigh escapes him as his shoulders slouch and his head droops. He stares at the ground while Angelina takes a seat beside him.

"I've often wondered which is harder," he says, "being you or being me."

Angelina stays quiet, not wanting to influence, giving him space.

He fidgets on his seat, folds his arms, squeezes tight, leans forward without breathing, and then he rushes on. "The moment I stop doing what he wants is when I become too high a risk for him." Again, he holds his breath.

Implications hang in the air like ripe cherries for those who can reach to pluck them.

After some moments, Angelina says, "Did you get the results from the blood test?"

Doc's head twists up to look at her but stops before their eyes meet; then, he turns back to study the ground under their feet. Eventually, he delivers his reluctant response.

"It was Adam's."

"He couldn't have known that!" Angelina says, trying to restrain herself.

"No, he didn't. After leaving you with me that evening, the test wasn't complete when he called. He didn't even ask for the DNA results. Told me to perform the procedure regardless. Immediately. I don't know why. But, if he knew it was Adam's, he would have told me to do it anyway."

"Why wasn't he there when you killed my mother?" she says, her tone hard.

Surprised again, Doc's eyes meet Angelina's this time, and after another long pause, he answers.

"He … let me say goodbye to her, alone."

Face scrunched up, he stares at her. A tear trickles down his cheek. His ever-smoldering pain reflects an unexpected pure quality in his otherwise putrid soul. In the pools of his water-filled eyes, she imagines smelling its lavender-like sweetness escaping the rank deposits of a shit-filled pond that should've been buried decades past.

Whatever else he is or has done, Angelina realizes, *having to kill my mother hurt him deeply.*

"You did it anyway?"

He nods and lowers his eyes slightly but carefully ensures that she can still see into them.

"I am weak. A coward ... and ... I know it's not an excuse, but she was lost, no matter what I did. Their relationship had become embittered. He'd switched his focus onto you. At least I could ensure she didn't suffer. That's what I tell myself anyway," he says.

"I loved her, your mother, like the daughter I never had or could have. When he ordered her death, it ... broke m ..." Doc's chin and lips scrunch up again; large tears run down his face.

They forget the plants and flowers as they sit, each bound in their world of whirlwinds hiding hungry, savaging monsters and dark clouds eclipsing unspeakable horrors, sharing a little of each other's suffering, yet with universes between them.

Eventually, Angelina says, "I think I'm ready."

Doc looks up at her, questioning.

"To take over from him. I'm ready."

"Are you sure that's wise? I think you might be underestimating what it may mean to you," he says, trying to be sure he's on the right track without asking or saying it outright.

"I'll end up a worse person if I continue like this. If I kill him, I can live my life how I choose. Become whatever I want to become," she replies matter-of-factly, confirming his suspicions.

Doc nods thoughtfully. However, a spark lights up within him, accompanied by a twinge of excitement and a rush of apprehension.

"Will you help me?" Angelina asks after a while.

"There's a lot to be said for loyalty," he responds, looking her directly in the eye again.

"But he's a monster!"

"And I am not?" he asks. "And you, what about you? Will you become a monster also if given the chance?"

"I fear I've already become that," Angelina mumbles, looking down.

Doc doesn't try to contradict her. "But I'm not finished. If I help you, the chance that you, by default, will question my loyalty will be high. There's a risk I might lose any security in my life," he says, observing her.

Angelina nods, constantly maintaining eye contact. "How old are you now, Doc?" she asks.

"I'm sixty-one plus forty-two. Why do you ask?" Doc started taking The Fruit two years after it came on the market after he'd studied the short-term effects of the drug on himself and many of his patients.

"Curiosity. What provides your security now?" she says.

"I'm not sure anymore," he answers, turning away, eyes wandering randomly. "The only thing I have to go on is safety in numbers. He hasn't removed me yet. Hopefully, the chance is less with each new year. And he knows my weaknesses. If he ever thought I'd betrayed him, I'd lose my life in a most horrific manner. He knows I fear that. How pathetic is that?" He huffs softly.

"Don't be silly!" Angelina says. "You're about as close to a friend for him as could be. He certainly doesn't have anyone else. On top of that, his father was disappointed in him; his wife let him down, or I believe that's how he sees it, and he probably thinks I've let him down. You've provided the only constant, trustworthy relationship he's ever known.

"No. He needs you, even if he doesn't openly acknowledge it," she concludes.

Doc doesn't respond; he doesn't know what to say. He shakes his head, disbelieving. Everything's wrong, and yet right, not only with her words, but with the facts. He's lived so long in this twisted relationship that is impossible to escape, save by death. Despicable.

"So will you help me despite the risks?" she asks again, openly not addressing his worries.

"Will you need me as much as he does?" he counters, smiling.

"I fear I'll need you a hell of a lot more," she smiles back and hugs him.

"Do you have a plan?" he asks.

"Tonight, we have our weekly dinner. You slip him something to sedate him, then we take him downstairs," she responds immediately.

"You know he'll be more cautious than usual. He'll know about our talk today," Doc warns.

Angelina raises her eyebrows and huffs lightly. *I should've known.*

"Then choose your moment carefully. I'll throw him off guard with a little present.

"Now, hang on," she says, opening a section in her handbag. Grinning, she zips open some well-hidden pockets and gingerly lifts out two plastic-looking long, flat, oval-shaped translucent strips and a thin but strong-looking gold necklace with a small round pendant.

"We can communicate using these. I'm wearing one, too." Angelina places the strips in his hand and opens the locket. A thin plastic see-through film on one side of the locket holds a small round disc in place inside it. "Extraction device," she says and snaps the clasp shut again.

"What do I do with these?" he says, waggling the strips.

"Stop that," Angelina says, frowning and grabbing his wrist, and she takes one of the strips from him.

Doc raises his eyebrows as she folds down his turtleneck and, on one side, places the strip on his skin just below the line of his sweater.

"Tiny prick," Angelina says and presses firmly. "Leave these in place. The build-up of cleansing chems can cause irritation at the entry point, so no scratching." Then she presses the second strip against the other side of his neck. "They'll be absorbed in a while."

"Oh, really?" Doc says, crossing his eyes, trying to see. "And this?" He holds up the necklace.

"Here," Angelina says and fastens it carefully around his neck. "If you ever need to remove the device, hold the disk's silver side against your neck, roughly centered where the strips are now."

He lightly places his fingers on each strip and closes his eyes as if imagining or memorizing.

"You must move it around until you hear a solid beeping sound. Then hold it in place until all beeping stops. You might feel a tiny prick: A retractable needle. It takes about fifteen seconds on each side. Use it in case of emergency."

Better not lose it then, he thinks.

"Now, the device should be ready after lunch. We'll test it then," Angelina says, then she stands, pulls Doc to his feet, and they continue their walk through the tropical garden.

With the cold winter's sun baking through the slanted greenhouse rooftop's lower half, they take in the last tropical sections while walking off their lunch. Angelina admires a massive display of jade vine hanging down ten meters from just under the highest glass panes.

"Magnificent," Angelina whispers, looking up. In the bright sunlight flickering through the trees, lighting up the multi-colored flowers, she stands in a tropical jungle filled with fierce sounds of nature, all capped under a heavenly blue sky. For a short while, she dares to imagine being free.

Doc patiently waits until Angelina sighs and turns to him. "I'll go over there.

You wait here. When I indicate, say, 'Answer.'" Then, moving about ten meters away, she calls Doc on his newly installed CCOTCHA.

He looks around him, confused by numbers and words that appear in his peripheral vision, and they remain in sight as he turns his head, scanning the garden while searching for the source of a beeping he hears. His gaze settles momentarily on Angelina. Making an urgent twirling movement with her index finger, she urges him to take the call, and finally, he focuses on her. "Answer," he says.

"Hi, Doc," Angelina says, smiling like a child with a new toy.

Doc's jaw drops on hearing her voice inside his head. "Sviatlana, what is this?" he asks.

He sometimes uses her original name when he's sure they're alone. "It reminds me of your mother," he told her once.

"It's called a CCOTCHA, a covert communication device. It's, er, stolen from the BITS Inspector's science partner. But it's reprogrammed and secured. Only you and I can communicate over these CCOTCHAs."

"You can hear me?" he says, even more surprised, clearly not thinking straight.

"Well, it's complicated, but yes. How else could we communicate? Now, listen ..."

She begins instructing him how to use the device, ready for the day's work ahead.

"OK, now we can stay in touch," Angelina finally says, once finished with the lesson. "We need to plan. Will you arrange something to drug him with?"

"Yes, yes, of course. But can we hang up from this contraption now? I mean, you're right here. Or there," he says.

"CCOSHUT," she says, laughing as she walks back to him.

"CCOSHUT?"

"Hmmm, yes. Forgot that part. Instead of 'CCOTCHA off.' I programmed our CCOTCHAs to shut down almost completely after thirty seconds of inactivity," Angelina says.

"*Our* CCOTCHAs shut down?"

"Yes. I have spares. Reprogrammed and deactivated so no BITS Inspector equipment picks up on them. But only you and I are actually wearing a CCOTCHA. Originally, the CCOTCHA stayed on by default, like a telephone, ready to use.

"Never wait thirty seconds. Always shut it down when you're finished. It sends out random signals that only I can find. I'll activate your device if I need you. You can start it again any time, as I told you.

"All signals and comms are sent on random frequencies and encrypted so nobody can intercept them," Angelina explains. "It's totally safe," she says as if she'd designed the pilfered gadget herself.

Angelina pulls a mini handheld Roboid from her handbag, turns it on, and waits a few seconds until it starts beeping. "I'm going to remove your ID chip."

Doc jumps back, raising his palms. Angelina chuckles.

"Don't worry. I've taken mine out, too. A long time ago. I also programmed the CCOTCHA to emulate your chip and its functions, so you can still pass through the Line safely. And my father can find you if he needs to."

Angelina studies the Roboid until it beeps again. The ID chip is ready for pickup. She places the curved end of the pistol-like device just above Doc's upper lip. Two small cone-shaped plastic-covered protrusions extend from the device, curving upwards a short distance into his nose. Completely painless. The only thing he should feel is the Roboid resting gently on his skin. After decades of evolution, her ID chip technology is so tiny it's almost invisible to the naked eye but still packs enough power to kill. The Roboid beeps three times when it's finished collecting the ID chip.

After removing and hiding the device, speaking gently, Angelina says, "Now, go home and prepare." She shoos him off to find his transporter, but then she has second thoughts. "Oh, Doc," she says, grabbing for his arm.

"Be especially careful of Boris. He's got eyes in the back of his head, that guy."

"I don't think you need to worry about Boris, my dear. I'm certain he's loyal to you," Doc says.

"My dad pays his salary, Doc. So, don't be so sure."

Before leaving, Angelina purchases a huge potted young flame lily plant from the tropical garden's shop, nodding when the man asks if she wants it gift-wrapped. Waiting outside the exit, Boris sees Angelina and comes in to carry the plant for her.

Wise choice to wrap it, Angelina thinks as Boris tucks it under his arm, the paper covering the leaves brushing his face as he follows her to the limo. *Or I could be driving him home.* And she chuckles inwardly.

At the old family mansion, Angelina avoids her father like the plague. She plans to surprise him with a long-awaited good mood. And the longer he waits, the bigger the surprise. She hopes an exuberant beaming smile will throw suspicion on the deadly plant and that he'll worry she's trying to poison him with it.

Staying out of his way is easy enough. Being technically gifted, Angelina hacked into Val's surveillance system years ago. Watching the comings and goings was fun initially, but keeping tabs on his whereabouts now is more of an exception than a rule.

Her recent captivity and the related events had motivated Angelina to brush up on her surveillance skills. She'd watched the recordings of what happened to Adam. And, while searching for these, she'd realized there were numerous locations she didn't have access to, and others, she found, were pre-programmed with periods of constant fake images at inexplicable times.

It took a full seven days to satisfy her curiosity. She uncovered areas unknown to her in the maze of computers and data that her father had secured with not-so-hard-to-crack keys. Not so hard if you knew him, that is. And she found a host of data and recordings meant only for her father's eyes.

These findings confirmed Angelina's previous suspicions about Val, and more.

Angelina had recognized that her father had become increasingly perverted over time. Her younger decades were happy enough. She was naïve, adored him, and enjoyed being with him.

But later, she began to see through his lies, to sense the darkness behind his desires. And she worried that in his very core, something terrible was amiss.

She came to realize he'd designed her very existence to suit himself, indeed, her whole life. But she also saw that he had no one else except Doc, so he was pitiful, and she felt trapped. And so, she rebelled.

In the search for herself, she moved further apart from him until he eventually tried to manipulate and later force the love he needed from her. And with each year, she felt his escalating dominance more acutely, as an increasing assault against her very sanity.

Yet not even in her angriest of moments did she consider he could've murdered her mother to suit his own needs, to keep her to himself.

When Angelina understood her father took her mother from her, a lifetime of longing and misery washed over her once more. Where was the one person that she needed and missed the most, the only one in the universe destined to carry her to birth and bear her? Did she never love her baby? Was her baby just a burden? Was she not compelled by heart-strung bonds to care for her baby? *What terrible thing did I do to make you leave me?*

She endured Doc's twenty-one-hour grieving over his beloved lost Alena, watching him watching her dead mother. And delirium came over her. A madness inflamed by a merciless mishmash of frenzied memories and emotions enough to send any average person over the brink and on to the next life. She didn't smash or break anything, didn't rant and rave or scream and shout.

She sat silent, staring.

Angelina's long years of agonizing converged and exploded in an ungodly rage that ravaged her mind and whipped her feelings into an ever-wilder fury. They whirled so fast that a reaction so toxic turned her soul to a swirling molten core, fiercer and hotter than the undying sun itself. It boiled the rivers of her blood like lava, ready to erupt without a moment's notice.

CHEATING DEATH

"Tata," Angelina says, her beaming expression warming the mood as Val fails to hide his surprise.

She hasn't properly smiled since Adam died. And the last time she called him Tata was in their good years.

Questioning him with raised eyebrows, Val turns to Doc as if he should explain. But Doc shakes his head and shrugs.

Angelina nudges the door closed with her hip, then rushes the wrapped package in her arms over to the large oak table at the far end of the lounge. It's clearly a plant, even for those who didn't know: Paper bulging out at the top, chunky and round at the bottom, tell-tale signs of earth.

As she crosses over to them, Angelina observes Doc and Val sitting in their solid brown leather armchairs, like so-called gentlemen in a smoking-room scene from a century past. A low table between them holds their heavy whisky tumblers.

Bastards, both of them.

Val stands, arms reaching out, and Angelina hugs her father, brushing her cheek against his. He leans back, assessing her with a squinting, sideways glance.

"I'm feeling a lot better today. Happier," she explains, her smile aimed at his eyes. "I even went for a walk with Doc in my favorite garden. I do love that place.

"And I brought you something," she says, taking Val's hand. "Come. See," and she tugs him across the room.

"Let me pour you a drink, Angelina. Vodka?" Doc asks, following Val's every move.

"No, I'll join you with the whisky, thanks."

Doc reaches for his drink as he stands. His deceptive hand passes over Val's whisky and drops in a tiny pill before picking up his own glass. He sips his liquor while watching Val suspiciously eying his present.

"Now, Dad, this one is *quite extraordinary*," Angelina says, exaggerating to make a point. "You'll need to be *extremely* careful with it."

Doc replaces his glass, stealing a peek at Val's tumbler. No sign of the pill. *Good. As easy as that—if he drinks it.*

Removing the wrapping paper, Val brushes against a leaf with the side of his hand. Angelina grabs his wrist and pulls it away.

"Don't touch it, silly. Even doing that can cause irritation," she warns.

"Silly me, indeed. Fine present to give your dad, a poisonous man-killing ... what ... baby triffid?" he says.

"It'll only kill you if you eat it," Angelina says and laughs.

"It can do that?"

"Oh yes. So, find something else if you suddenly get peckish. But it's quite beautiful in flower."

"Now, Doc, where's my drink?" she demands playfully, meeting Doc halfway. He dutifully hands over her tumbler. "Can we sit for a moment before dinner? I'm a little tired," Angelina asks, looking at her father.

"Of course, Angel. Let's toast your return to good health," Val says, and with an expansive wave, he guides Angelina toward the sitting area.

Their glasses clink, and they drink. Angelina sits opposite her father, who can't seem to prevent himself from scanning the full length of her legs.

"It's so nice you've joined us this evening," Val says, trying to fill the silence.

Angelina smiles, but the massive sofa aggravates her solitude, and she sees Doc observing her. Setting aside her loneliness, she focuses on those wandering eyes to stoke the burning anger ravaging her veins. Fury is her only comfort now, but she's careful to hide it well, for his gaze pierces deeper than he lets on.

"Tell me about this garden," Val says. He hates small talk. So does Angelina. But it's safer, for now, he hopes. "I've never been there. It sounds like an interesting pl ..."

Val's mouth hangs half-open, his eyes flashing up, left, right as if searching. Then he stands abruptly and waves an arm in the air. If one were to guess, one might think he was trying to point at something specific. Or someone. But he fails miserably.

"Ya ..." Val mutters, then his knees crumple under him, and he falls to the floor.

"Oh my god!" Angelina exclaims.

Doc jumps to his knees beside Val and lays him out, arms and legs straight.

"Doc, what's happening?" Angelina asks in a panic.

"Don't know. Get security. Tell them to bring a gurney from the surgery."

Angelina calls Boris.

Doc checks Val's condition thoroughly, knowing it'll be some minutes before the stretcher arrives. The surgery is downstairs in the vast underground basement between the medical research labs, the gym, and the swimming pool. Angelina also has one of her creative rooms down there. Her escape room she calls it, away from the rest of the world.

Boris arrives fast with two Serpents. No stretcher. Val' doesn't allow monitoring of the private video from the drawing room, but the guards are always on call close by.

Within ten minutes, they move Val down to the surgery. Four nurses hurry about, changing him into a hospital gown and installing life supports, monitors, and drips. Val had kept the medical team in the house after Maksim passed away. They double as Doc's research assistants in his lab work and help with his patients.

Doc instructs the nurses from Val's bedside. Two Serpents stand guard at the door, looking helpless. *Not helpful.*

Boris had instructed his Serpents to bring an armchair from the basement lounge beside the gym. He stands beside Angelina, who sits watching her father. Val breathes mechanically on the doctor's table; Doc tells them his condition is stable but critical.

"I'll scan him. But we probably need to get him to hospital," he says.

Advanced scanning methods combining ultra-scanning, advanced computer, and Bitsi-Lite wireless tech can provide highly accurate insight into someone's condition. But seconds into the scan, all the monitors start beeping loudly.

Two nurses fire off a sequence of checks as Doc bawls a list of instructions; two more nurses scurry around Val, doing everything possible to revive the dying man. Doc shocks Val's heart with a defibrillator but to no avail, and after some time and many attempts at resuscitation, he finally accepts defeat. He looks up at the nurses, who confirm the conclusion with simple eye movements and small nods of heads. Turning to Angelina, he simply shakes his head slowly.

Angelina slumps deeper into her comfy chair. She presses her hands against her face, tries to hold away her tears. Silence replaces the beeping, broken only by the nurses' clicks and clunks while clearing away. But before they remove the drips, Doc intervenes.

"I'll do the rest. Please leave us now." Walking over to Angelina, he says, "I'm so sorry, my dear. I'll call in a medical examiner immediately. We'll try to ascertain what happened," his tone deep and quiet.

Angelina grasps his pale, mushy palm with her firm, long-fingered hand. With the other, she pats his wrist. Recognizing his loss, she stares into his eyes for a moment and nods a few times, still weeping. It's easy for her to call upon the tears: She has many reasons to cry.

"You should all go now," Doc says, turning to Boris, then looking around at the other Serpents. "Remember, Angelina is your charge now, your concern.

Her safety is *your* responsibility. Your loyalty is to her now," he declares, pupils small and eyes focused while delivering his message and studying their reactions. He dismisses them with a shove of his chin toward the door.

"Of course," Boris says.

The Serpents say, "Ma'am," as they bow their heads at Angelina and then leave the room. But Angelina calls out.

"Wait! Please move my chair over beside him," she says while standing up. "I will sit with him a while."

The chair is heavy, and it takes two men to move it. Doc crosses the corridor and enters the small lounge beside the gym. Stocked with some of the best liquors money can buy, it's sometimes used for relaxing after exercising or as a retreat. He calls the Serpents to move a small table to Angelina's side, then takes a glass and a bottle.

"Would you stay with me for a while, Doc?" Angelina asks.

"Of course, my dear." While pouring, he says to Boris, "No one must come down here unless explicitly requested." Exchanging nods with him, the Serpents leave the room again.

"Just give me a moment, Angelina," Doc says and rushes out. "Boris," he calls out.

Boris stops and turns, raising his eyebrows.

"I'll switch off these cameras for now," Doc says, indicating the devices with glances, a pointing finger, and a flick of his head. The surgery, gym, lounge, and corridor. Angelina's escape room. More than a handful in all. "I don't think she wants anyone watching her right now." He pulls up the surveillance on his phone.

"Of course, Doc," Boris responds.

"Oh, hang on while I speak with the examiner. Let me do that first." Doc finds the details for his acquaintance, the city coroner, knowing the medical official works late hours. The man answers the call immediately.

Boris watches Doc's every move. It's in his nature to observe. It's also part of his job.

"I need to call in that favor," Doc explains once the brief niceties are over. "Yes, now. I'll send a car over if that's OK?" Doc asks rhetorically.

The conversation started and ended before the coroner even began to wonder what it was about. Not that it mattered much. He wouldn't dream of refusing Doc's request to repay a favor.

Doc harrumphs as he hangs up, looking at Boris. "The coroner. Annoying man, but he owes me. And I'll not have Val bullied about in that shabby morgue. Those people don't care about the dead."

"He has a reputation," Boris says, raising an eyebrow.

"Oh, but he's quite brilliant. So long as he keeps his shaky fingers away from the living. He can tell us what happened."

Something in Doc's sly smile makes Boris wonder, but he doesn't interrupt him.

"I'll meet him in the drawing room when he arrives."

"I'll send a car," Boris says.

"Tell him nothing at all. I'll do the talking. Oh, and make sure there's cognac in the car. It's quite a drive."

Boris nods, then marches off after his Serpents.

That was easy enough, Doc thinks, expelling a huge silent sigh on his way to the gym lounge's bar. Before tackling the cameras, he pours a stiff drink to calm the remaining jitters. Then, having double-checked that the Serpents and nurses have vacated the basement, he returns to the surgery with a whisky refill in hand. He crosses straight over to Angelina.

"Cameras?"

Doc nods.

Chinking their glasses together, Angelina says, "Well, that was easy," and tries to laugh. She doesn't pull it off. Instead, she yaps once like a puppy dog that's had its treat confiscated.

"Be thankful for that, my dear. I don't dare even think of the consequences if this went wrong," he says. "I think I've just knocked five years off my life. I've never done anything this dangerous before."

"Did you change the password on these cameras?" she says while chuckling.

"I did."

"And restart them to check?"

"I did. And then I shut them down again and checked that, too."

"Good. Show me," she demands, not unkindly.

He expects no less; she's always been careful. He reaches for his phone, and she pulls a small, thin cigarette case from her slim-fitting pants pocket.

"And I'll just smoke this," she says, pulling a marijuana cigarette from the small, flat silver box.

Doc barks a half-laugh as she offers him one. "This once, I'll make an exception."

All the cameras are indeed off.

Grimacing after his third toke, Doc gives up and deposits his glowing reefer and whisky glass on the surgery's scrub sink. He hates smoking of any kind, and it's been decades since his last attempt. Only the urge to celebrate this short, bizarre interlude between eras spurred him into taking the joint. It's not a sense of freedom that elates him; he's equally trapped regardless. But there's a wave of excitement surrounding this change, and he intends to ride it as much as he dares. It could be his last opportunity.

"I'll fetch the plastic. Take your time, my dear," he says. He can't tell whether she hears him or not.

He quickly finds what he's looking for, standing in a tall cupboard in the corner of Angelina's escape room. Where she'd said they were. The plastic is taller than he is. *Wallpaper?* he thinks as he wrestles two rolls to the floor, leaving the last two in the cupboard as instructed.

He heaves the unwieldy cylinders into the surgery one at a time, banging against the door and frame, cursing quietly under his breath. If Angelina notices, she doesn't let on. Not until he drops the last roll to the floor. Then she stands and lays her joint on the scrub sink beside Doc's, unfinished, like his. She wanted to feel the drug's release, but she also wants her wits intact.

Angelina eyes the long rolls laid out on the floor. "It wasn't easy getting this stuff in," she says, bending down and pulling at some tape. "So many cameras. I piled a ton of wallpaper on top—like I planned to redecorate. Hah! As if I'd ever do that," she laughs. Then she pulls two tape dispensers from a cupboard she'd hidden there earlier, and they start work.

When finished, the drop cloth covers almost everything from waist height and down, including Val's gurney, the room's centerpiece. Val lies on the plastic, naked, his head, legs, and arms bound and strapped around the chest. They piled his remaining scalpel-shredded clothes in a corner.

Angelina takes a short break. With eyes closed, she rests back in the comfy chair that now stands behind her father's head. She sips her vodka while Doc wraps black tourniquets loosely around Val's upper arms and legs. He tugs the straps gently, then releases them, testing that they work.

"That should do it," he says.

"Ready?" Angelina stands and walks over to inspect his work. The plastic crackles and scrunches under her feet.

"Yes. And I've decided, if you don't mind, I don't think I'll stay in here."

"Whatever you want, Doc," Angelina replies, reaching out and lightly touching his forearm. "I'll only need an hour or two. Once I start, it'll be hard to go slow."

He nods. *It won't be fast for him,* he thinks. "I'll message you when the coroner arrives. Remember, tell me when it's OK to come down. And nothing on the face and hands." He kisses her gently on the forehead.

Before leaving, he turns and looks around the room. In that moment, he doesn't see Angelina or Val, the gurney, or the clean plastic drop cloth.

He experiences time. A countdown.

Anticipation greater than he's ever known. The approaching end of a disastrous year or century. No, era. And the beginning of new resolutions. Like planning the violent felling of the so-called cruel Egyptians to herald in the triumphant rising Greeks and *their* so-called glorious gods. It's as if Doc sees the wonders of a new universe revealed for the first time, drawing closer, endless possibilities within his grasp—once this new era ushers in.

He won't miss the old. Won't miss Val, his only reason to hate and to feel constant fear. Yet he's afraid to look too closely at the new. Ever afraid. For now, he just hopes.

He shakes his head, closes the door on his past, and takes the hidden passageways up to Val's bedroom and closet to find clothes for later.

Finally, alone and looking down on her father, Angelina's face slowly reveals the true emotions stirring within. Her lips curl up, opening slightly, tips of white teeth showing like a cornered and angry wild dog's—ready to snap and rip. She focuses on her victim, the skin around her glowing eyes stretching back, camouflaging her secret fear of failure and its consequences. Fear of her own weakness. If she were to utter a sound, it would surely be a vicious growl.

She pushes in Doc's plunger, millimeter by millimeter, her piercing gaze alternating between the drip and Val, watching for the smallest of movements as the drug enters his system. Nothing.

Wake up, you bastard.

Removing the syringe, Angelina throws it unceremoniously across the room, and it clatters into the scrub sink. Then she sits in the chair behind him, crosses her feet, and, using a remote, she sends a huge hovering TV to the end of her father's mobile bed. And she waits.

Shit. He said this would be quick. And she watches. *Oh my god, I hope he's not dead.*

Val finally stirs, and within the next minute, he's fully awake, alert, and frantically tugging on his restraints. They're tight enough to prevent any movement, further fueling his rapidly accelerating anger.

"What the hell? What is this? Get me out of here!" he says. It's not obvious what he's thinking, except that he expects someone to heed his command.

He's clearly not aware of the coming new era. Not yet.

Angelina flicks on the screen. A picture of her mother lightens up the room, and Val stops shifting and struggling against his bindings.

"What the …?"

Pressing the remote, Angelina kicks off her carefully prepared slideshow. Key moments in Alena's life. Clothed in her first baby outfit after returning home from the hospital. Her baptism, playing on the lawn—a flash of white panties covering her crotch, the chrismation, her first confirmation. All bright, gay, happy memories.

Val looks on, fixated. Under different circumstances, he'd probably smile. Now, he barely breathes.

The first day of kindergarten, then school: Private lessons with personal teachers all held within the confines of the grand old mansion. There are not many pictures. Now, a snapshot of a distraught twelve-year-old Alena crying over her big brother's shoulder, her father, Maksim, lying on his deathbed. The last slides are of Val and Alena's fake marriage and Sviatlana's birth. Alena still looks like an innocent angel at sixteen despite her years of abuse.

A tear trickles down Angelina's face. It burns hot.

"Where did you get these?" Val calls out as the last photo fades away. He tries but fails to see behind him.

"You gave them to me, Tata, remember?"

Val's mouth drops open as he sucks in a quick, quiet gasp. *You? First, Adam. Now this, you ungrateful bitch,* he thinks, and his head droops as he imagines her plan.

Angelina steps out from behind the bed. Val glances first at his daughter, then at the sword hanging by her side, one hand teasing the hilt.

"What do you plan with that?" he asks, recognizing the way she's fondling the weapon.

She ignores his question. He is no longer in control here. "You gave me everything I have," Angelina says. "And I hate what you gave me."

The sharp ice in her voice cuts chills down his back. He shivers.

A soundless video plays on the screen. Angelina has prepared highlights of the evening her father murdered her mother. It opens with the message exchange between Val and Doc.

Val flashes a frantic look at Angelina, but then he fixates on the screen. *She's found everything,* he thinks. He panics, yet he watches, mesmerized. *Now she has everything I have.*

"You gave me my life—and I hate you for that."

The demon driving her begins prowling the room. The blade's cold steel hisses in the still air as she draws it from the sheath that protects everyone from its razor-sharp edge.

Val knows the sound well; from far off, he senses the sun setting on a bygone era. He shakes again, this time, uncontrollably.

"And you could take life from me. Just as you took life from my mother."

The video runs, silently jumping from one moment to the next. Angelina raises the sword above him, across the bed. Val's eyes flit from her to the blade and back. She takes in his every movement, can taste his angst, and revels in the stench of his fear.

He tightens his muscles when she lays the gleaming Samurai steel flat across his belly. Then, slowly drawing the sword's edge along an invisible mark, she opens a blood-red precision line a millimeter or so deep. Val clamps his jaw tightly shut, grunting through gritted teeth as she slices.

But he's strong, and he's coped with physical suffering in the past. By the time the short video finishes and Doc has stopped crying over Alena, and the funeral ends, Val's regained his self-control.

"She was going to leave me and take you with her. She was going to take you away from me! I didn't have any choice," he blurts. "I didn't want to lose you. And I thought I could give you a better life with me."

"I don't agree with you, Tata," Angelina says, her voice deep and rasping. Val stares at her, his expression a rare vision of horror as she twists around, glances at his feet, and raises her sword to one side.

The faint whistle of steel cutting air lasts but a moment.

Swinging her glistening blade diagonally, she slices off his pinkie toe with the razor-sharp tip. Val's savage, agonized scream fills the room. Blood spurts from his open wound, splashing and rat-a-tat-tapping on the crisp new plastic.

Angelina raises her arms again, swipes down, and Val roars. The second stub shoots a small spray of blood, and the third toe hangs loose, half off. She overshot, and briefly moves closer to check. A few stray red drops splatter her face.

Stepping back again, she swings, and he wails. The third toe falls and bounces on the drop cloth. No longer trying to escape his bonds, Val grips the gurney for dear life.

Twice more, she wields her blade, and Val's primal, anguished yells could conjure chills reminiscent of ancient times when terror was first invented. Nothing remains but a straight line of stubs. Blood shoots and oozes sporadically from his open arteries.

Angelina sheathes her sword, yanks on the tourniquet around Val's lower leg, and then turns away. His eyes frantically search her out, as if seeing what she's doing might make this easier. Leaving her father grunting and moaning, Angelina crosses over to the long wall-side cupboard. She takes up her phone, sees that the coroner has arrived, and messages Doc that he can come down—but to come now. A few minutes and a few sips of vodka later, Doc reports that they've reached the lounge.

Good, now I can finish this. Malice twists her face into a scowl.

If she has a plan at all, it contains only three elements: End his life, inflict as much pain as possible, and enjoy herself doing it. *The bastard has it coming!*

Angelina plays the recording of her fiancé's murder.

Val's screams and cries had reduced to a pathetic, intermittent whimpering. But seeing his face on the big screen again, he begins crying out once more.

"Angelina, no! No more! What can I do to make it up to you? Angelina?"

Further down, on the wall-side cupboard is a metal tray with basic surgical utensils. Angelina selects the scalpel and a large pincer. *If you have any last words,* she thinks, *then now's the time.*

Stretching his eyes to the left, he watches her every move.

As Angelina walks over to him, tools crudely displayed in her hands, it's anyone's guess which part she'll grab with that pincer and where she'll start to cut.

He doesn't ask. "No! Angelina, stop! Nooo!"

But she neither cares nor waits. She's had enough of his honey-coated lying and his crying; enough of the sound of his voice.

She holds his nose, forces the pincer between his lips—doing her best not to mark them—then grips his tongue, squeezes, and pulls. Val yells a blood-curdling scream as he realizes what's coming.

With two careful cuts and a final tug to rip off those last tricky sections, she pulls his flapping tongue from his mouth, clamped between the metal prongs.

Angelina releases the strap around her father's head, and he immediately turns, gurgling and howling to one side, spitting out his blood. She slings the scalpel, pincer, and tongue toward the scrub sink. They hit the surface with a clack and a thud and smack up against the back wall. She barely notices.

Val holds his breath as he watches Angelina draw her sword, sneering viciously. The slow hiss of metal against sheath dominates the deathly stillness. Then she turns toward his other foot. Val's eyes follow as she braces and raises to swing, and he screams. "No!" A base, muted gargling sound.

She glances at him, lips parted, twisted. A monstrous growing savagery ravages Angelina's captivating beauty. And Val sees the new era dawning just over the horizon.

BE CAREFUL WHAT YOU WISH FOR

"So, Doc, best tell me what this favor is you wanted," the coroner says. "If I drink much more of this fine brandy, I'll not be fit for anything." He smiles unabashed, takes another eager gulp of his favorite tipple, and then swipes away the spill trickling down his chin. The ever-present redness and blotchy skin betray him.

Doc has endured small talk for over an hour with this blabbering incompetent drunk, struggling with his infamous slur that for decades further darkened his already tainted reputation. That's what made it so easy to buy his services. But he's old-school and knows his stuff. He exercised significant influence once upon a time, and that will help when it comes to spreading the word.

He has *drunk enough,* Doc guesses and glances at his old-fashioned wristwatch. *Let's get this done.*

"Ah, yes. Well, an unfortunate incident with my boss has left me needing to complete a postmortem," Doc says.

"Oh dear," the coroner says, his tone flat. He stares intensely at Doc.

"Don't worry. You don't need to do the examination," Doc says.

"Thank God!" the man exclaims. "You know how I bloody hate doing those things. If it weren't for my little friend here," he says, hugging his bottomless buddy, "I'd be up top, mingling with the best of them." His eyes momentarily focus on a distant place, his pitiful smile presumably reflecting a dreamy life in the upper-middle-class medical society, way above the chilled basements of the dead.

"Most certainly," Doc lies. "Now, I did a quick autopsy myself if one could call it that. Such a simple affair: Clear-cut case of severe myocardial infarction. All I need you to do is sign the documents witnessing the death certificate," Doc explains, holding out a tablet computer.

The drunk looks at the screen. An arrow on the medical form's last page clearly indicates where he must sign. "You don't even want me to verify your findings?" he says, somewhat uncertain.

"Good lord, man! You think I don't know what I'm doing?" Doc says.

"Don't be daft. Of course, you do!" the coroner says and focuses his gaze on the small screen. He doesn't read the document or even check who the deceased is. He simply scribbles his scrawl on the digital death certificate.

"Thank you. Now Angelina can get on with the business of preparing her father's funeral."

"That was the great Valentine himself I just witnessed?" the coroner says, raising his eyebrows, wary again.

"Who did you think it would be? I'd not otherwise be involved in something like this myself," Doc responds, pretending to be mildly affronted.

"Yes, yes, of course," the official says slowly, the crease of his brow deepening further.

But a strange look comes over Doc's face, and he reaches into his white coat for his phone, logs into a camera, and studies Angelina at work. Then he shoves the video feed in front of the coroner's face.

"And this is the stunning Angelina," Doc says. "She will be even greater than he was."

Worry gives way to horror on the coroner's blotched face. His wide-open eyes turn to Doc as he realizes his life is now bound to his silence, and Doc's slightly nodding head confirms it.

He'll talk. Eventually, Doc thinks. *That's what drunks do. The coward won't expose himself, but he'll tell a fine story. The stuff of legends. And she will be feared.*

Ten minutes later, he deposits the coroner back in the drawing room where he'd found him. He instructs security guards to take him home, then returns to the basement lounge to relax. And wait.

Doc startles and wakens. More than an hour has passed. His phone vibrates as a second message from Boris arrives. Responding to Boris, Doc then sends a message to Angelina: You OK? But after pacing for some minutes and getting no reply, he checks the security camera.

Standing over her father, Angelina raises her sword high and brings it down hard into his chest. The blade sinks so deep that she struggles to remove it as she prepares for the next stab. Her fierce motivation wanes as exhaustion gains the upper hand. But why she continues Doc's not sure. One more stroke won't change anything now. Val has clearly been gone a while.

He studies Angelina for a moment. *She's lost it,* he thinks, and pushes himself up from his comfy armchair using both hands. As usual, fear of the consequences of inaction conquers his fear of action, and he heads out the door and across the corridor.

"Sviatlana, it's over," he says, closing the door.

She looks up, but he can't tell if her unseeing eyes recognize him. Val's blood covers Angelina's hair, face, arms, and upper body: Sticky, dark patches, more brown than red. An expression so cold and unmoving, yet so vague. Then, focusing again on her father, Angelina heaves the sword high.

"He killed my mother," she explains to Doc as if he didn't know it. "He killed my fiancé," she grunts as she pierces Val's dead belly. Then, straining once more, she pulls, his flesh and skin lifting slightly as the sword sucks free. She raises its hilt skywards one more time.

"You'll never fuck me ... or hurt me ... again," Angelina says, her tone a tired snarl, and she grunts and stabs.

Relying on Angelina's regular, if not tired, rhythm, Doc takes his chance while she safely sinks the blade into Val's abdomen. He steps beside her, ensuring she sees him. "Sviatlana!" he calls out quietly.

Her terror-struck gaze meets his, and he fights off a shiver.

"It's over, my dear," he says again, wrapping one hand around her lower arm and gently placing his other palm on the nape of her neck, carefully avoiding thick blood patches. His drug-cocktail plasters concealed in each hand contain a small, potent dose of sleeping drug.

Double, for safety. Ever careful; ever the coward.

"Half an hour of sleep will do you a world of good, my dear," he says. While she looks at him, grasping at his words, her eyes glaze over, and she collapses in his arms. He drags Angelina to the plastic-covered comfy armchair, gently lays her down to rest, then removes the drug patches.

Guess I'll clean this up myself, he thinks, looking around and smiling. *Small price to pay.*

He assesses the work ahead. The blood spill concentrated around the gurney. He can't see any splashes that have strayed from the plastic, except for by the scrub sink. *Just patch up, fix the drop cloth, and dress him for the funeral.* Doc runs through their plan as he looks around. Then he nods and starts work.

One by one, he picks up each limb from the floor and sews it back on with a rough stitch using thick black thread from a sewing kit he'd prepared earlier. *So it doesn't accidentally fall off.* He smiles happily as he stares at the grotesque skin patchwork.

God, I can't remember ever feeling this good, he thinks, grinning. *I'm practically free! Free as I want to be.*

Engrossed in his work, Doc loses any sense of time and planning, and he's surprised once he finally finishes reconstructing the last leg. *Nothing more worth sticking back on,* he thinks, throwing the remaining small body parts in the sink. The waste disposal unit crunches loudly as it chews on the bones. A liberal dose of acid sizzles as it burns away the remaining evidence.

Every now and then, he glances at Angelina but concludes each time that he's doing fine and that she deserves the rest. So, he lets her sleep. He cuts the plastic from under Val and goes about the business of washing his hair, face, and hands, ready to dress him in his Sunday best.

While he surveys the results of his work, he suddenly blurts out a half-barked laugh. "Hah!" *Even Frankenstein didn't look this good.* And he chuckles at the thought.

"You seem happy," Angelina says, smiling at him from across the room.

Doc leaps almost out of his skin, threatening to become the second case of severe myocardial infarction in the building within twenty-four hours.

"Oh, my dear, you made me jump!" he says.

She smiles widely, quietly laughing.

Good, she's back, he thinks, rather relieved. *It could've been awkward if she'd completely lost it.*

"How long have I been out?" Angelina asks.

"Just a few hours. I, er, gave you something to help you sleep. It's three forty-five, and all we need to do is dispose of this drop cloth, switch gurneys, dress him, and apply the finishing touches so he's ready for viewing," he tells her.

"Oh, Doc. You did all that yourself?" she says.

"It's quite all right, my dear. As you noticed, I rather enjoyed myself." He grins at her. "I feel almost young again. But he's dehydrated. We'll need clever makeup to disguise that," he says, serious again.

"My department," she smiles.

"You should shower first, my dear. I'll do what I can in the meantime."

They don't talk about what happened or how she behaved. They look to the future with an unspoken mutual agreement, knowing they'll soon bury the past. Literally.

"I'll be as fast as I can," Angelina says.

When Angelina returns from refreshing herself, Doc has the drop cloth rolled up and stashed onto the trolley. They transfer Val to a new hovering bed, then, under the cover of faked camera images—courtesy of Angelina—they wheel the gurney, bloodied plastic, and clothes down to the back of the mansion.

The great furnace greets Doc like an old friend, and he reciprocates with a smile while pushing the trolley inside. Even the gurney frame melts quickly under the fierce heat of those powerful gas burners.

While returning to the surgery, they recover the funeral clothes Doc stashed earlier in Angelina's escape room. Then, struggling with the heavy torso, they push and shove Val into the chic black polo neck sweater and black suit, ready for the last ceremony he'll ever attend.

At five-fifty-five, Val's makeup and hair are in pristine condition, and he's ready for the coffin.

"You get some sleep, Doc," Angelina says. "I'll take a nap here. See you at nine?"

Within an hour of the news of Val's passing, the police paid a hasty visit to Angelina. Doc and Boris stood by to support her, a handful of Serpents supporting them.

"Has the cause of death been established?" the detective asked, looking down on Val, all dressed up.

"Heart attack," Doc said. "Here is the death certificate, witnessed by the coroner."

The officer raised his eyebrows, took the device, and studied the document. "That was fast."

"We go way back," Doc said. "And we are both in the business of helping people."

The naturally suspicious man stared intensely at him before turning to Angelina. "And where were you at the time of his death?"

"She was taking aperitifs with her father and Doc in the drawing room. Whisky, if you must know," Boris said.

Angelina's eyes flicked over to Doc, then to Boris for a fleeting moment, but if Boris saw, he didn't show it.

The detective gave Boris a short nod. Those two also go way back.

"I'll keep this," the detective said, hefting Doc's notepad in his hand. "It'll save me some paperw…"

In a single fluid movement Angelina swung her sword from its sheath and pressed the straight, razor-sharp tip up under the left side of the man's chin, just enough so it didn't cut.

Boris drew his gun, and his Serpents followed suit as the junior detective reached into his coat. Stretching out a detaining hand, the older policeman brought his colleague in check.

Angelina scowled at the detective, eyes glaring, then she clenched her jaw, and shoved the blade a few centimeters farther under his chin. A hairline cut.

"Here," the detective said, and handed back Doc's device.

Angelina lowered her sword and jerked her head violently toward the door.

"Let me take a look at that for you," Doc said grasping the detective's elbow and, with a flick of his head at the junior officer, he led them away, the Serpents following. "Nasty shaving cut, that."

As Doc closed the door, they heard him saying, "If you value your life, don't ever…"

Later that day, they held an open casket funeral facilitated by called-in favors and promises of considerable contributions to the local church, undertaker, and catering firm. It was a small affair. Only Val's immediate household attended, along with one member of the press and the closest of Val's friends, those who could adjust their busy schedules.

Doc made all the arrangements, or so they made it seem. He explained the need for speed as a matter of respect for Val.

"Don't want him lying up here all alone among the living. He'll be much happier beside his father." *And we want the bastard rotting in hell as fast as possible.*

That was bogus, of course. Upon Val's request, according to Angelina at least, they cremated his body. But she never planned to bury his remains. Angelina took the ashes home and flushed him down the toilet in his bedroom. *Where he belongs.*

Lawyers arrived to read the will just hours before the funeral. Everyone jumps when such big money is involved. Angelina was the only person whose presence was necessary, together with Doc, who served as a witness. The will was short and straightforward, and the reading took less than half an hour. Val left everything to his daughter.

Angelina and Doc excused themselves for a short while during the wake. A different law firm read the will for the underground affairs, but it was the same drill and also over fast.

After the last guests leave, Angelina heads directly to the large drawing room. She takes Val's painting off the wall, lugs it to the back of the house, and stashes it in an old, rickety cupboard behind the great furnace. Back in the lounge, she studies the now-empty space beside Maksim's painting. *Not going to fill it. I'll have to get used to it,* she decides, just as Doc enters.

They'd agreed to skip dinner that day, so now Angelina and he can finally relax in the lounge's luxurious comfy chairs. Angelina sighs and smiles, sipping on a vodka. Doc takes his pleasure in a sweet Black Russian.

"I do love that sweet coffee-rum combination with the sneaky backhanded lash of vodka," he says dreamily.

"I've never heard you speak of enjoying something before. Even something that simple," she says.

"Ah, if only that could continue forever," he replies.

There's still a loosely formal air to their relationship, but there's also something new. Something born of a shared need stemming from a lifetime of soul-distorting oppression under Val's domination over them. A need fostering a hidden yet desperate longing for escape or release. An elemental desire to experience life on their own terms.

Yet, Angelina had never been alone and wasn't sure she could. Doc knew he couldn't.

So, as if each of us lives in our own bubble that none can break into unless we allow it, and we cannot break out of unless we fight for it, so, a new bubble formed around them both. Binding them forever.

Their mutual cocoon comprised blankets of protection, awareness, companionship, past fears and pains, and secret future hopes. It created a complex affinity based on empathy and filled them with newfound compassion toward each other that bordered on being humane even though they were both undeserving monsters, and their growing strength in this new oneness also provoked their evil natures.

"Nothing lasts forever," Angelina says, her tone cold.

Doc huffs and studies her face.

In a roundabout way, he's part of Angelina's inheritance. But they haven't properly discussed his future yet. So, Angelina takes this opportunity to ask what he wants.

"I would hate returning to the cliquey medicine circles. I don't think I'd even survive normal society. I'm sure someone would have me locked up," he says, smiling sheepishly.

"No. Considering my skills and tendency to explore areas often deemed illegal, I think staying on this side of the law is best. But working for the competition is unthinkable.

"If you feel you can for… well … if you could use a personal physician, I'd love to stay on with you."

"I cannot forgive you—if that's what you meant. But I do accept that he coerced you." Her harsh tone makes him shudder.

"Nevertheless, I'm relieved that you want to stay," she says. And it was true. "You've taken care of me since I was a baby … and … well, I would rather not … lose you."

Doc shudders again, his eyebrows raise ever so slightly as he bows his head.

"Thank you. I tried, Miss." His quiet voice crackles. "But ... he was rather headstrong, your father."

"As am I, Doc. Don't expect your work for me to be any easier," Angelina replies.

She stands and paces, contemplating her next words. Doc's attention falls momentarily on the samurai sword at her side, gently swaying in rhythm with her steps. She's carried the weapon since they left the basement with Val, he realizes.

"I have big plans. My father was not ambitious enough. Genius, maybe; ruthless, yes. But his twisted emotions limited and flawed his vision. He could neither see what was truly possible nor how to maximize his opportunities. I will *not* let that happen to me. And I'll need *you* to watch out for me in this."

Oh dear. "I'll do whatever I can, Angelina," Doc replies. *But if it happens, there'll be absolutely nothing I can do about it.*

Angelina lets out a deep sigh, then breathes in deeply again. Standing tall, she places one hand on her hip and sticks out her chin, looking at a point far into the future. Her sword sticks out behind her as she rests her other hand on its hilt.

"I want to go truly global," she states. "More continents, countries, and underground centers. Each independent, of course.

"And more areas of business. This time, we'll use the kosher organizations also as bait and hook, not only cover. And when they bite, we'll drag them down underground with us."

"Won't that increase our risk of exposure?" Doc asks.

Angelina nods while pressing on. "That's why each center must be independent, acting as safety nets."

She draws her sword just centimeters from its sheath, eyes glowing and mouth slightly agape as if seeing its destructive qualities for the first time. Doc raises his eyebrows and stares.

"We're going to be busy. There'll be hard decisions to make. Ugly competition. But those who choose to stand in my way should not do so lightly," Angelina says, studying the shining steel. *Because fresh red blood is my new favorite color.*

"In each region, we'll identify the illegal businesses, find the bosses, and overrun them all. But they mustn't know it's happening until it's too late.

"After that, expansion will come naturally. Attracting clientele will be a walk in the park.

"I will find everyone who ever had a dirty or unholy thought, even in a nightmare or a passing wish. I'll exploit their weaknesses and lure them into dreamscapes they'll pray they'd never experienced, for they will know there is no escape."

Hmmm, so be careful what you wish for, Doc thinks, and he shudders.

Angelina's gaze settles for a moment on Grandad Maksim's portrait, but then she sighs, bends to pick up her glass, and gulps down her vodka.

"Boris, where are you?" she calls out in a harsh tone.